The DIVER'S
H A N D B O O K

The DIVER'S HANDBOOK

Alan Mountain

The Lyons Press

First published in 1996 by
New Holland (Publishers) Ltd
London · Cape Town · Sydney · Singapore

The Library of Congress Cataloging-in-Publication
Data is on file.

ISBN 1 55821 552 2

Senior Designer: Peter Bosman
Editor: Anouska Good
Publishing Manager: Mariëlle Renssen
Illustrator: Steven Felmore

Australian Consultant: Barry Hallett
British and Cold Water Diving Consultant:
  Lawson Wood
Medical Consultant: Dr Cleeve Robertson
Technical and Training Consultant: Mike Clark

Reproduction by cmyk prepress
Printed and bound in Singapore by Tien Wah Press
  (Pte) Ltd

10   9   8   7   6   5   4

PUBLISHER'S NOTE
Diving is inherently dangerous, and the
advice and instructions in this book are not
intended to take the place of a formal
program of diving instruction offered by
licensed instructors as described in Chapter 4.
No one should attempt any form of
diving without successfully completing
such a program.

Author's acknowledgements

I would like to thank Mike Clark, one of South Africa's best qualified and experienced divers who introduced me to diving some 30 years ago, for the valuable advice and support he has given me in writing this book. I would also like to thank Dennis King for his advice on the marine environment. Finally, a big thank you to my diving buddies, particularly those in Durban, who have helped to make diving such a pleasurable experience for me.

Publisher's acknowledgements

The publishers would like to thank Jaco Smit of Scuba Venture for his invaluable assistance during numerous photo shoots. In addition, we are extremely grateful to Underwater World and Orca Industries for allowing us to photograph their equipment, as well as the Two Oceans Aquarium for the use of their facilities. Lastly, we would like to thank Rob House for his work on the initial design concept for this book.

CONTENTS

CHAPTER ONE

A BRIEF HISTORY OF DIVING

EARLY BEGINNINGS

The need for man to descend below the surface of the sea for military, salvage, recreational or hunting purposes extends deep into the mists of antiquity. Nobody today can say when this first happened, although historians believe that it probably occurred some 5000 years before the birth of Christ. The earliest recorded depiction of a man diving under-water, however, is possibly that of a diver on an Assyrian relief that dates back to 885BC. An early authentic record of diving can be found in the writings of the Greek historian Herodotus, who told the story of a diver named Scyllis employed in the fifth century BC by the Persian king, Xerxes, to recover sunken treasure.

Most early diving was done for military reasons. Alexander the Great used divers to remove obstacles that had been sunk in the harbour at Tyre, which he had taken after laying siege to the port in 332BC. It is claimed that the great military leader actually went underwater himself to view his divers' work.

Records also show that in the first century BC there was an active salvage industry situated around the major ports of the eastern Mediterranean. The business was so well organized that a wage scale for divers, which recognized a pay differential for depth of work, was established in law. All diving was done by holding the breath; training began at childhood and these ancient divers developed stamina and

A diver loses his helmet and his life in Simonstown harbour, South Africa, 1906.

huge lung capacities. Flat stones were used as weights and guiding devices to steer the diver as he descended. A common practice was to tie ropes around the diver's waist so that co-workers could haul him back to the surface with the salvage he had managed to snatch from the dive site, which often lay 22–31m (70–100ft) below the surface.

An Assyrian frieze which is believed to depict a diver in the Euphrates River breathing from an airbag.

Klinger's dive suit, c.1803.

EARLY TECHNOLOGICAL DEVELOPMENTS

How to stay underwater for periods longer than human lungs could sustain was a problem that beset divers from the very beginning. At first hollow reeds were used but divers could only go down to the depths to which the reeds could extend. Their main use appears to have been in warfare when soldiers needed to cross rivers undetected. Records show that attempts were made to use longer tubes, sometimes with a diving hood attached to the end, as a sort of primitive demand valve which, in theory, would enable the diver to breathe freely. However, there are no records of these devices actually being

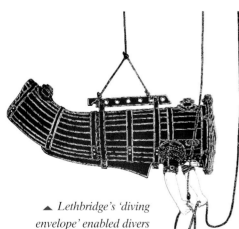

▲ *Lethbridge's 'diving envelope' enabled divers to work underwater.*

▲▲ *Alexander the Great used a glass barrel to view proceedings underwater.*

effective as it is unlikely that early divers had the materials and capacity to overcome the problems of pressure associated with depth underwater. Even at a shallow depth of 0.3m (12in) the pressure exerted by the water on a diver's chest is strong enough to prevent normal respiration.

There is a fair record of inventors in the 16th and 17th centuries who endeavoured to design apparatus which would enable individual divers to breathe freely underwater. Various drawings were published, but the designs were deficient and the dream of independence underwater continued to remain just that. However, in the later part of the 16th century the first breakthrough was achieved in the form of

an open-ended diving bell which was weighted and lowered vertically into the water, thereby entrapping air within the inner apex. This gave divers a reservoir of compressed air from which they could draw. The diver either remained in the bell or made breath-holding sorties from inside it. The first reference to such a diving bell was made in 1531 and from that time on they were used on a regular basis. In the 1680s, an American, William Phipps, used a system of 'mother and daughter' diving bells which enabled divers to have access to a number of air sources. In 1690, the English astronomer Edmund Halley designed an intricate system of replenishing the air in a diving bell by connecting its air supply to smaller diving bells (or up-turned 'buckets of fresh air') which were lowered beneath it. Once in place, a valve on the bucket was opened and the greater pressure on the bucket (due to its greater depth) forced the fresh air into the operator's diving bell, thereby replenishing it. Halley, accompanied by four other men, demonstrated the effectiveness of his design by remaining at a depth of 18m (60ft) in the River Thames for one and a half hours.

In 1715, another Englishman, John Lethbridge, developed a 'diving envelope' which encased the diver within a leather-covered 'barrel of air' equipped with a glass porthole for viewing and two armholes with watertight sleeves which enabled the diver to work underwater. The entire apparatus was lowered from a ship and manoeuvred into place in the same manner as a diving bell. Lethbridge was, from all accounts, amazingly successful in salvaging a wide range of items from a number of wrecks. In 1749 he wrote a letter to a popular magazine in which he recorded that his normal operating depth was around 18m (60ft) and that, at that depth, he could stay underwater for 34 minutes. However, his equipment suffered from the same limitations as the diving bell – a lack of manoeuvrability and an inability to provide a continuous supply of fresh air.

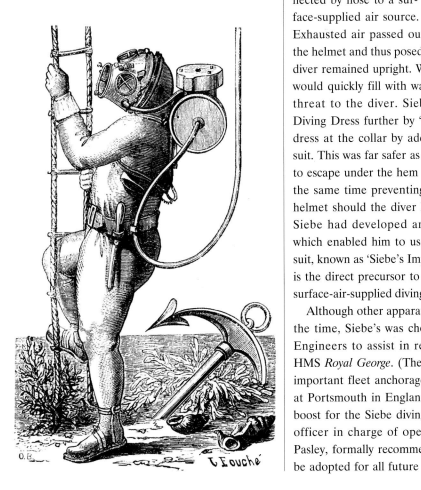

Salvaging items from wrecked ships was a lucrative business that provided a continued incentive for new inventions in diving techniques and equipment. Augustus Siebe has been credited with the first practical diving dress, but in fact he was only one of several men who were experimenting with very similar diving innovations at the time. John and Charles Deane, two brothers who were active in the salvage business, secured the patents in 1823 on a design for 'smoke apparatus' intended for use by firemen. After five years of further work, they developed 'Deane's Patent Diving Dress'; this consisted of a heavy suit for protection from the cold and a leaded helmet, with viewing ports, which rested on the shoulders of the diver and which was connected by hose to a surface-supplied air source. Exhausted air passed out from under the edge of the helmet and thus posed no problem as long as the diver remained upright. Were he to fall, the helmet would quickly fill with water posing a considerable threat to the diver. Siebe developed the Deane Diving Dress further by 'sealing' the helmet to the dress at the collar by adding a waist-length diving suit. This was far safer as it permitted exhausted air to escape under the hem of the diving suit, while at the same time preventing water from entering the helmet should the diver lose his balance. By 1840, Siebe had developed an effective exhaust valve which enabled him to use a full-length waterproof suit, known as 'Siebe's Improved Diving Dress'. This is the direct precursor to today's standard deep-sea surface-air-supplied diving dress.

Although other apparatus was being developed at the time, Siebe's was chosen by the British Royal Engineers to assist in removing the wreckage of HMS *Royal George*. (The vessel was obstructing an important fleet anchorage just outside the harbour at Portsmouth in England.) This provided a major boost for the Siebe diving system, especially as the officer in charge of operations, Colonel William Pasley, formally recommended that the Siebe dress be adopted for all future naval diving operations. It

▲ *Halley's Bell c.1690 enabled divers to remain underwater for extended periods of time.*

◀ *Rouquayrol patented the first demand regulator in 1866.*

is interesting to note that the official government historian who recorded the salvage and removal of the wreckage of the *Royal George* also commented that divers working on the job, which was done in six to seven hour shifts, at a depth of between 18–21m (60–70ft), reported repeated attacks of 'rheumatism and cold'. Colonel Pasley and his men were unaware that it was not rheumatism, but rather a diving disease that would only reveal itself several years later – decompression sickness, also known as 'the bends'.

THE DISCOVERY OF DECOMPRESSION SICKNESS

At first, decompression sickness was known as **caisson disease** because its occurrence was particularly noticeable among caisson workers. 'Caissons' (derived from the French word for 'box') were used in projects such as the excavation of bridge footings or the construction of tunnel sections and were constantly supplied with compressed air. They provided dry working conditions underwater for labourers who used to work eight-hour shifts, or even longer. As more and more construction projects requiring underwater work were tackled, so the disease came into ever-greater prominence.

It was the caisson workers on the Brooklyn Bridge project in New York who gave the disease its descriptive name '**the bends**'. It is probably the best-known sickness associated with diving.

A French physiologist, Paul Bert, undertook extensive research into decompression sickness, and in 1878 discovered that breathing air under pressure forces quantities of nitrogen to dissolve in the blood and body tissues. Should the pressure be suddenly released, the nitrogen returns to a gaseous state too quickly to pass out of the body in a natural manner. As a result, bubbles of gas form throughout the body and these cause the pain that the early divers and construction workers associated with rheumatism.

To overcome the problem, Bert recommended that caisson workers and divers return to the surface slowly and this led to an immediate improvement in worker health and a reduction in fatalities. Bert also found that the effect of the bends could be immediately relieved by increased pressure and this led in 1893 to the construction of the first recompression chamber in America. It was used to good effect in the construction of a tunnel under the Hudson River, between New York and New Jersey.

THE DEVELOPMENT OF DIVE TABLES

Bert's recommendation that divers ascend slowly did not solve all the problems faced by divers, however. Decompression sickness continued to plague divers who tried to work below 40m (130ft) for any length of time and it was also found that their efficiency deteriorated, with some divers eventually losing consciousness.

An English physiologist, J.S. Haldane, conducted a number of experiments with Royal Navy divers between 1905 and 1907 and found that the problem was caused by divers not ventilating their diving helmets adequately; consequently, high levels of carbon dioxide built up which steadily poisoned the diver. To solve this problem, Haldane recommended an increased steady flow of fresh air into the diver's helmet, measured at the pressure (depth) of the diver. Haldane also composed a set of tables which established a maximum bottom time at different depths and a staged method of decompression as the diver ascended. Although Haldane's tables have been re-evaluated and modified over the years, their underlying principles still form the basis of the accepted method of bringing a diver to the surface.

One of the consequences of Haldane's findings was the ability to increase diving depths to slightly more than 65m (210ft), the maximum depth to

▶ *A diver prepares for salvage work on a wreck in 1870.*

▼ *The underwater world has long been a subject of myth and legend for humankind.*

◀ *An early photograph of a surface-air-supplied diver at work on a wreck.*

▲ *Inflatable vests for buoyancy were typical of diving in the 1970s.*

which the hand-pumps of the day could pump air. However, at depths of about 30m (100ft) or deeper, a new malady began to manifest itself: a feeling of euphoria which affected divers in strange ways. Often all sense of responsibility seemed to vanish. This syndrome came to be known as 'raptures of the deep', today termed **nitrogen narcosis**. Its cause was diagnosed in the 1920s and found to be the result of the anaesthetic properties of nitrogen when breathed under pressure.

Amateurs and professionals continued to be fascinated by the lure of the deep and many attempts were made to perfect diving equipment which would enable divers to reach ever-greater depths. One line of endeavour was to produce reinforced diving suits able to withstand ambient water pressure and thereby enable the diver to breathe air at normal atmospheric pressure.

It was argued that by eliminating the effect of pressure on the diver he would be able to descend to great depths. Initially, however, it was not possible to produce a suit strong enough to withstand the effects of water pressure and flexible enough to be usable. This situation continued until around the 1960s when modern versions such as the Jim Suit and the Newt Suit were developed.

▶ *The experimental 'Nemo' submersible capsule was developed by the US Navy.*

▼ *An artist's impression of Otis Barton's 'bentoscope', a kind of deep-diving bell.*

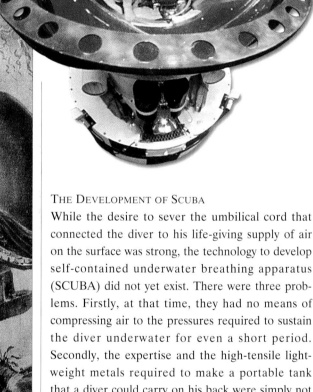

THE DEVELOPMENT OF SCUBA

While the desire to sever the umbilical cord that connected the diver to his life-giving supply of air on the surface was strong, the technology to develop self-contained underwater breathing apparatus (SCUBA) did not yet exist. There were three problems. Firstly, at that time, they had no means of compressing air to the pressures required to sustain the diver underwater for even a short period. Secondly, the expertise and the high-tensile lightweight metals required to make a portable tank that a diver could carry on his back were simply not available. Finally, they had no means of reducing the air pressure that would have to be contained in a diving tank to a level that would be usable.

However, it was only a matter of time before man eventually found the answer to independent movement underwater. This came about with the advent of Scuba equipment. Over the years, three basic types evolved: closed circuit, semi-closed and open circuit (see Chapter Three).

The development of the necessary components that make up the Scuba dive system did not take place simultaneously. The first demand-regulator, designed to regulate the supply of air from surface-supplied diving equipment, was patented in 1866 by

Benoist Rouquayrol. It was later adapted for use in the Scuba system. In 1878, H.A. Fleuss developed the first commercially viable closed-circuit self-contained underwater breathing apparatus. It used 100% oxygen which meant that smaller volumes were required for normal breathing (air contains only 21% oxygen) and the need for large lightweight high-strength diving cylinders was thus eliminated. Fleuss's system soon ran into trouble however, because at that time it was not known that 100% oxygen breathed under pressure becomes poisonous. By the time World War I broke out, a modified demand regulator had been added and diving cylinders capable of holding oxygen at more than 200 bars (30001b/sq in) had been developed. With these modifications the Fleuss self-contained closed-circuit diving system became standard escape equipment for Royal Navy submarines.

A French naval officer, Commander LePrieur, constructed a partially successful open-circuit Scuba system using a reinforced tank of compressed air. However, most attention continued to be focused on developing closed-circuit diving systems, despite their practical limitations and the constant risk of oxygen poisoning. During World War II closed-circuit systems were used by both sides, but two Frenchmen, a naval officer and an engineer, worked at developing an open-circuit Scuba system. Captain Jacques-Yves Cousteau and Emile Gagnan, working under the restrictive conditions of German-occupied France, brought together hundreds of years of progress in underwater diving to develop the first safe and fully efficient open-circuit Scuba system. It was they who developed the first *aqualung* which Cousteau used to successfully glide down to 60m (200ft) with no ill effects.

After the war, the aqualung became a commercial success. As a result of the diving comfort and ease that the open-circuit system offers, recreational diving has become one of the fastest growing sports in the world. It has also made it possible for marine biologists, geologists, archaeologists and a host of other scientists and researchers to explore and reveal some of the sea's many mysteries.

▶ *The one-man 'Spider' submersible is one of many systems being developed for underwater exploration and scientific study.*

CHAPTER TWO

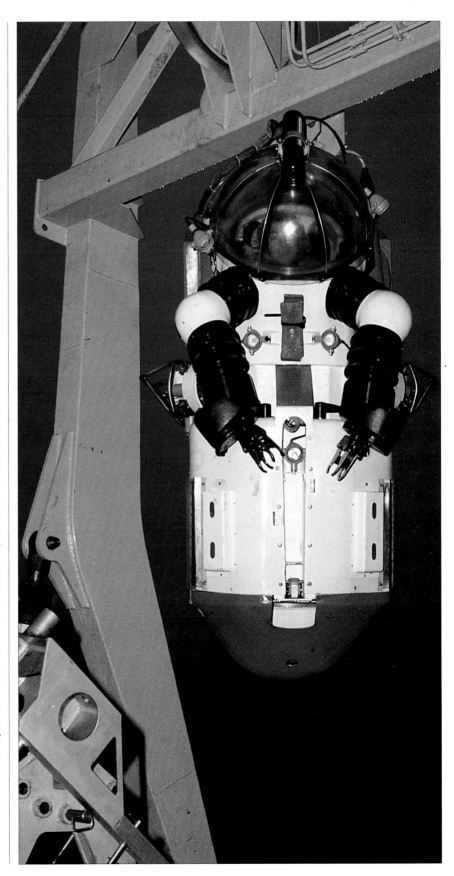

THE NATURAL LAWS OF DIVING

It is important for the diver to know the natural laws that govern the principles of diving. Without this knowledge, it is difficult for the diver to understand the reasons for rules which must be observed if the sport is to be safe. It is vital that divers understand the differences that exist between air and water environments. Obvious differences include the following: the increased viscosity and density of water enables those who venture underwater to enjoy one of diving's great thrills – weightlessness and the ability to move in the third dimension; differences in acoustic properties make communication difficult underwater; differences in optical properties result in changes in appearance of objects with regard to their colour, size and distance; and differences in the heat capacity of water result in a constant exchange of heat between the diver and the surrounding water, thus placing great strain on the heat stores of the human body. The less obvious, and therefore perhaps insidious, differences are the effects of pressure on air breathed at depth and the resulting physiological effects on the diver.

MOLECULAR STRUCTURE OF WATER

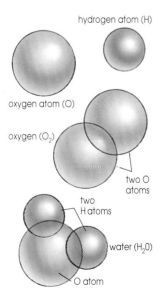

hydrogen atom (H)

oxygen atom (O)

oxygen (O$_2$)

two O atoms

two H atoms

water (H$_2$O)

O atom

THE NATURAL LAW OF MATTER

Most recreational divers breathe compressed air, a form of matter made up of a number of gases with oxygen and nitrogen as the primary constituents. Air also contains small amounts of water vapour, trace gases (such as argon and neon), carbon dioxide and various hydrocarbon pollutants. The normal ratio of gases in the air we breathe is approximately 78% nitrogen, 21% oxygen and 1% other gases. However, some advanced divers and those diving for commercial, scientific or military reasons may use specially blended gas mixtures, known as *Nitrox* or oxygen-enriched air. These have different

Diving confidence comes from understanding the natural laws that govern the principles of diving.

RATIO OF GASES IN AIR

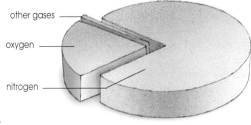

concentrations of nitrogen and oxygen and are used for particular diving situations, such as staying underwater for extended periods and to decrease the risk of decompression sickness.

Nitrogen is a colourless, odourless and tasteless gas but, despite being the major component of the earth's atmosphere, the human body does not use it physiologically. Nitrogen can pose certain risks when it is breathed under pressure as it may result in nitrogen narcosis and decompression sickness.

Oxygen, like nitrogen, is also colourless, odourless and tasteless, but is an essential ingredient for life. Many of the body's chemical reactions need oxygen in order to generate the heat and chemical energy required for them to take place. However, for divers the right volume of oxygen in the air is critical since too much or too little can cause serious problems.

Carbon dioxide is colourless, odourless and tasteless too. It is a major component of exhaled air and its concentration within the body sends a signal to the brain to set the breathing apparatus in motion. An excess of this gas is potentially dangerous.

Carbon monoxide is a poisonous, colourless, tasteless and odourless gas that forms as a result of the incomplete combustion of hydrocarbons in internal combustion engines. It is normally exhausted into the atmosphere; however, if the intake of a diving compressor picks up these exhaust fumes while the Scuba cylinder is being filled it could be highly dangerous as carbon monoxide seriously impairs the blood's ability to absorb oxygen.

In order to know what effect the presence of different gases in air has on diving, it is necessary to understand the relationship between those gases and how this relationship changes due to pressure. For this we need to understand **Dalton's Law** on partial pressures which states that:

▼ *The design of Scuba equipment is based on the natural laws of diving.*

In a mixture of gases, each gas exerts a pressure proportional to the percentage of the total gas which it represents.

In other words, the whole is equal to the sum of its parts. In air there are approximately 21 molecules of oxygen in each 100 molecules of total gas; thus oxygen exerts about one-fifth of the total pressure. This fraction of total pressure is known as the **partial pressure** of oxygen and is an important factor in diving, since the human body is more directly influenced by the partial pressure of the different gases than it is by absolute pressure.

THE NATURAL LAWS OF PRESSURE

Scuba equipment is designed to take account of the natural laws of pressure. Pressure is the force that is exerted when molecules collide with each other. If a gas is squeezed so that the molecules occupy a smaller volume, the number of collisions increases and the pressure also increases. This occurs when diving cylinders are pumped with air. Increased volumes of air are squeezed into the same physical area and as a result the molecular impact in the cylinder increases. The same situation exists with the gaseous atmosphere around the earth. If it were possible to cut out a column of air equal to 2.5cm² (0.4 sq in) extending from sea level to the outermost layer of air and weigh it, it would tip the scales at 6.7kg (14.7lb) or **one bar**. Thus one bar, or 14.7lb/sq in (14.7psi), is described as 'one atmosphere of pressure absolute' and is the weight the human body is subjected to at sea level. Therefore, the higher we ascend, the greater the reduction of atmospheric pressure – for example, at 5000m (16,400ft) above sea level atmospheric pressure is reduced to half its weight (0.5 bar or 7.35lb).

Once we descend below the sea's surface the reverse happens. Pressure increases at a rate of 1kg/cm² for every 10m (14.7lb/sq in for every 33ft) in sea water. Thus one additional atmosphere of pressure (one bar) is experienced for every 10m (33ft) of sea water (or 10.03m [34ft] of fresh water). Accordingly, on the surface of the sea atmospheric pressure is equal to one bar, at 10m (33ft) below the sea's surface it doubles to two bars, at 20m (66ft) it trebles to three bars, and so on.

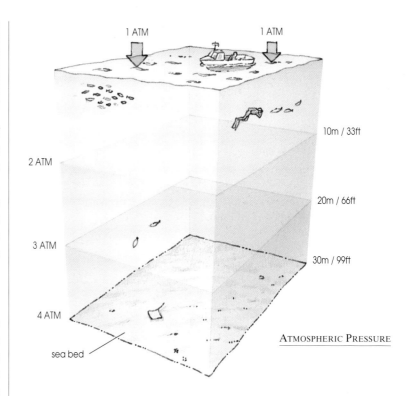

ATMOSPHERIC PRESSURE

Depth gauges measure pressure, not water depth. Essentially a depth gauge is a mechanical (or digital) device that converts measured pressure into depth readings but there is a difference between **gauge pressure** and **absolute pressure**. Normally, pressure gauges are calibrated to read zero at sea level but the atmospheric pressure at sea level is already one bar, therefore, gauge pressure reflects the increase in pressure from a base of one atmosphere (one bar) and is normally designated as one bar(g) – bar (gauge) – or 14.7psig (14.7 pounds per square inch gauge). Absolute pressure includes atmospheric pressure. It is thus the true pressure on a diver at any depth (the sum of gauge pressure and atmospheric pressure), and is designated bar(a) – bar (absolute) – or psia. Depth gauges are only accurate if they are used in the environment for which they have been calibrated. If a depth gauge which has been calibrated for sea level is used at altitude the readings are likely to differ from the actual water depth. Thus, for altitude diving, a well-calibrated zero-adjusted depth gauge should be used in order to ensure correct readings. A factor to be taken into account in altitude diving is that it is invariably done in fresh water; therefore 3% of the gauge reading should be added to compensate for this.

▲ *A knowledge of science, nature and history is often required in diving.*

Recognizing the existence of innate pressure in the atmosphere and in water, we need to examine the behaviour of gas under conditions of changing pressure and temperature. To do this it is necessary to understand two natural laws; the first is **Charles's Law**:

If pressure is held constant, the volume of gas will vary directly with its absolute temperature.

An axiom to this law is that if the volume of gas is held constant the pressure will vary as temperature varies. Because of this, divers should never leave their full diving cylinders in direct sunlight or any other heat source for any length of time. As the temperature increases, pressure builds up in the cylinder which could be dangerous, particularly if there is any cylinder wall weakness. The next very important law to understand is **Boyle's Law**:

The volume of a gas varies inversely with absolute pressure while the density varies directly with absolute pressure, provided the temperature remains constant.

This means that as pressure increases, the volume decreases and as pressure decreases, the volume increases. This inverse relationship can be calculated using the mathematical formula:

$$P_1V_1 = P_2V_2$$

where V is the volume of air delivered by the cylinder and P is the ambient pressure at depth. For the diver, the significance lies in the fact that the deeper he or she descends, the greater will be the volume of air required to equalize the air spaces in the body and to breathe.

Since the diver must breathe air at a pressure equal to that of the surrounding water, a mechanism is required not only to reduce the higher pressure of air in the diving cylinder to the diver's lower pressure requirement, but also to be able to do so at different depths. The regulator system intrinsic to Scuba is designed to accomplish these tasks as it adjusts the volume of air drawn from the tank to accord with the diver's depth. The deeper the diver descends, the denser the air that he breathes becomes and, since the regulator's inflow mechanism is balanced by ambient pressure, it accordingly allows more air molecules per unit of volume to flow through to the diver. This effectively reduces the amount of air that is available for use in direct proportion to depth or absolute pressure.

The relationships between pressure, volume and density are very significant for the diver. During descent, pressure increases and pushes inward on all body air spaces. If these spaces are not equalized, a condition known as **squeeze** results and this normally affects the ears, sinuses and diving mask. The lungs are not affected by squeeze as long as the residual volume is not compressed. Should this occur, it could cause segments of the lung to collapse.

During descent the lungs will compress and reduce in volume, but they will expand again on ascent and return to their original volume on the surface. In the case of skindivers, some of the air in the lungs will be used to equalize the air spaces in the body as there is no external air source. The lungs will therefore be slightly reduced in volume as the diver reaches the surface. Great care must be taken by Scuba divers as they ascend to see that they constantly breathe out, since a diver breathing compressed air must permit expanding air (due to reduced pressure on ascent) to escape. Failure to do so can produce several forms of lung barotrauma (see Chapter Five).

BOYLE'S LAW

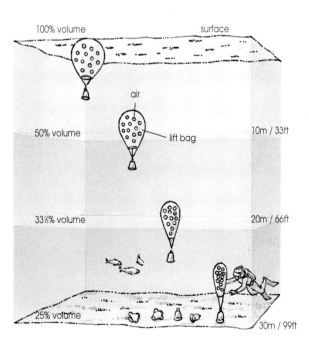

100% volume   surface

air

50% volume   lift bag   10m / 33ft

33⅓% volume   20m / 66ft

25% volume   30m / 99ft

THE NATURAL LAW OF BUOYANCY

When an object is partially or wholly immersed in a liquid, it is buoyed up by a force equal to the weight of the liquid displaced by that object (Archimedes' Principle). This means that items less dense than water will float (known as **positively buoyant**), while denser items will sink (**negatively buoyant**). Items of the same density will neither float nor sink but simply hover in the liquid (**neutrally buoyant**). There are thus three factors that are involved: the weight of the object, its volume and the density of the liquid. For divers, Archimedes' Principle has an important implication: that of ensuring that the diver achieves controlled or neutral buoyancy throughout the dive. The diver is subject to a number of forces. If he or she is too light, the buoyancy of water will either keep him or her afloat or will make it difficult to descend and maintain depth. If the diver carries too much weight, this may make it difficult to move about in the water and to ascend. Both are tiring and dangerous as the diver will constantly battle against the forces of gravity if over-weighted, while if he or she is under-weighted, the diver will have to overcome the upward forces of buoyancy through hard leg work. Besides the added physical exertion required, the exhilaration of gliding effortlessly through the silent underwater world is lost. To assist the diver in achieving neutral buoyancy, an essential item of equipment is a **buoyancy compensator** (see Chapter Three) which must be used in conjunction with the correct amount of lead weight.

It is important to note that to dive safely and to progress to more challenging and advanced levels of diving, these basic natural laws must be fully understood and never forgotten. In the same way that a driver has to learn and remember the basic rules of driving and road safety as well as be able to apply them automatically, so too should a good diver know the basic rules of diving.

▲ *Good divers will always maintain a level position.*

CHAPTER THREE

EQUIPMENT

In order to dive successfully it is essential that you know your equipment well and that you are familiar with all of its idiosyncrasies. Comfort is also an important consideration. A thorough knowledge of your equipment also means that it is easier to pick up potential problems more quickly, and thus you will hopefully be able to prevent them from occurring. It is important to take care of your equipment and to have it regularly serviced.

There are three Scuba systems: open-circuit, semiclosed-circuit and closed-circuit. Of these, open-circuit systems are usually used by recreational divers, although there is a move among some of the more experienced recreational divers to use semiclosed-circuit diving systems.

An open-circuit demand system is one where the diver inhales air from the diving cylinder and exhales directly into the water. Closed-circuit systems are also known as rebreathers as they remove the carbon dioxide from exhaled air and add oxygen as needed. Thus the same air is continually rebreathed by the diver and no air is expelled into the water to give off the tell-tale bubbles that accompany open-circuit systems. This makes them particularly attractive for scientific and military use. Semiclosed Scuba systems recycle part of each exhaled breath while allowing some gas to escape into the water, giving greater endurance and bottom time. These systems are used mainly by scientific and commercial divers, and the military.

It is vitally important for divers to blend in with the underwater world if they hope to experience rewarding encounters with marine life. Movements should be restrained and unhurried, and time

Many fish are inquisitive.

should be taken to observe the passing scene. Breathe slowly and steadily and avoid unnecessary actions. Fish of all sizes are often curious and may well come to inspect you if you do not frighten them away.

A diving gear bag is a useful item of equipment as it enables the diver to keep all of his or her diving gear together and in one place. Gear bags should be sturdy and large enough to accommodate all equipment, excluding the diving cylinder and weight belt which should be managed separately.

THE WELL-EQUIPPED DIVER

It is essential that a diver is well equipped at all times and that equipment is properly cared for. Divers should be thoroughly acquainted with how their equipment functions and should be ready to cope with any emergency situation that may arise, including equipment malfunction.

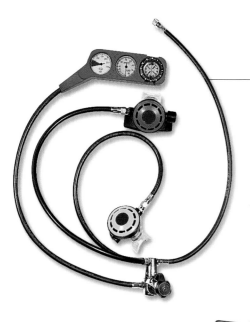

A regulator with instrument console, two demand valves, BC connector hose and a first stage.

Weight belts are used to counter positive buoyancy.

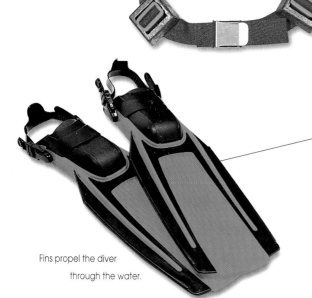

Fins propel the diver through the water.

Today, mainly single high-pressure tanks are used for diving.

Buoyancy compensators (BCs), or buoyancy control devices (BCDs), are inflatable bladders which are commonly jacket-styled.

A dive slate is useful for conveying messages.

compass

depth gauge

pressure gauge

Torches not only light up dark places but also reveal true colour underwater.

The mask provides clear sight underwater by providing a window and air space in front of the eyes. Snorkels are used for breathing on the surface.

A dive knife is essential for protection and as a tool.

Booties provide protection and warmth.

MASKS

The purpose of the mask is to allow a diver to see clearly underwater by maintaining an air space in front of the eyes and providing a 'window'. The air space within the mask is subject to the effects of pressure and must, therefore, be equalized underwater. This is always done during descent and is achieved by the diver blowing air through the nostrils into the air space between the face and mask. In order to be able to do this, the nose must be included within the mask.

Visual correction is important for those divers who require glasses. This should be taken into account in selecting a mask. For those who prefer to wear contact lenses, a low-volume mask with an excellent seal is necessary.

▼ *Masks should have a wide vision and allow as much light as possible to enter.*

Many different styles, colours and shapes of mask are available but it is important to note the following desirable features:

- Easy external access to the nostrils to facilitate equalization
- Strong retaining headband
- Wide field of vision
- Low volume
- Easy visual correction, if required
- Shatterproof glass
- Good double seal on the mask skirt.

It is important to test fit the mask before making a purchase. Place the mask against your face without using the strap and then inhale through the nose. The suction created should hold the mask perfectly in place for as long as you hold your breath. You should also test to see that it is possible for you to block your nose with your fingers and so be able to equalize pressure.

New masks normally have an oily film on the lens. This must be removed before use otherwise the mask will tend to cloud over, even after demisting procedures have been followed, until such time as the coating wears off. A good way to remove the oily film is to gently rub it off using toothpaste, both inside and out. Masks will always mist over naturally due to the difference between the temperature within the mask, caused by normal body heat, and the cooler water temperature. This potential problem can be overcome by spitting into the mask and rubbing the inside of the glass, or by using a commercial demister prior to entering the water. Before each dive it is important to check the mask's holding strap. Make sure that the mask fits snugly without being too tight and that the strap is properly secured with a locking device after adjustment. The latest masks are self-draining and can be cleared by exhaling through the nose.

SNORKELS

Snorkels are little more than reinforced plastic tubes fitted with a mouthpiece that enable the diver to breathe on the surface without lifting the head out of the water.

There are three basic designs: J-shaped, contour-shaped and those that use flexible hose for the bend. It is important to avoid long thin tubing (a good snorkel should have a diameter of about 2cm; 0.75in) and should be about 30–35cm (12–14in) long. To facilitate breathing, the diameter of the tube should be wide enough for you to insert your thumb, as this is more or less the same diameter as your pharynx.

Inevitably water will enter the snorkel and therefore it is important that divers breathe carefully in order to prevent water from entering their lungs. Water should be blown out regularly thereby avoiding the possibility of inadvertently inhaling it.

Factors to consider are fit, comfort and minimum breathing resistance. The only effective way of checking these factors is to place the snorkel's mouthpiece in your mouth, hold the barrel against your head in front of your left ear and breathe through it. The mouthpiece should be straight in your mouth and you should feel no resistance in your breathing.

▲ *Snorkelling is an easy way to enjoy the underwater world.*

The choice of snorkel is a matter of personal preference as, technically, there is very little to choose between the various types of modern snorkel.

FINS

In both Scuba and skindiving the main form of propulsion is achieved by kicking the legs. Fins, or 'flippers', provide a larger surface area which enables the legs to propel the body forward with relative ease.

There are two types of fins – full-foot fins and open-heel fins, both available in different sizes and designs. The most suitable fin is determined by the diver's size, physical strength and the diving conditions.

There are two important factors to be taken into account in selecting the best fins for your purpose: the first is blade size and rigidity (the larger and stiffer the blade, the greater the strength required to use it) and the second is whether you need to wear diving booties or not. In colder water where wet suits are worn, neoprene diving booties will help to prevent heat loss and, therefore, open-heel fins, which are designed to fit over booties, would be the most suitable. The same applies for dry suits where neoprene or stong rubber diving boots are an integral part of the suit's manufacture. In tropical waters, however, where it is unlikely that you will need a full-length wet suit and diving boots, full-foot fins would be most appropriate. Fin comfort is important, and, in the case of open-heel fins, it is vital that they can be properly adjusted.

Divers can choose between open-heel fins (top) and full-foot fins (above).

◀ *Even with fins, humankind will never be able to compete against the flippers nature gave turtles!*

BUOYANCY COMPENSATORS (BCs)

Buoyancy compensators (BCs), or buoyancy control devices (BCDs), are inflatable bladders which can be front-mounted, back-mounted or jacket-styled. The jacket-type BC is by far the most popular and universally used. The BC's configuration and harness arrangements should be comfortable and designed in such a way as to prevent the device from riding up and ending around the diver's neck when inflated. All controls should be simple, easy to locate and to operate.

BCs have become a mandatory piece of equipment because of the important role they play in diver safety. They are easily inflated, either by air from the diving cylinder, by mouth or from an alternate air supply. They are used to provide surface support for resting, swimming, assistance in holding an injured or sick diver afloat and for achieving neutral buoyancy underwater.

All BCs come equipped with a pressure-relief valve to prevent overpressurization of the bladder. The valve is held closed by a spring which has a tension of approximately 2psi. Should the internal pressure of the BC exceed this limit the spring will decompress and the excess pressure will be released. All BCs should also be equipped with a dump valve which allows for the rapid 'dumping' of air from the bladder. This is necessary on descent when air may be trapped in the BC, thus making the diver positively buoyant and unable to descend without overexerting him- or herself.

Some BCs incorporate a small air cylinder which can be used in an emergency to inflate the BC independently of the primary Scuba cylinder. The unit also has a demand mouthpiece that allows air in the bladder to be inhaled by the diver while exhaled air is exhausted into the water.

Using the BC as a breathing bag is an **emergency** measure **only** and requires special training, regular practice and a calm temperament.

The BC is a major component of the Scuba system and its use is mandatory. Comfort and durability must take preference over price.

▼ *Full-face masks provide minimally restricted vision.*

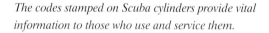

The codes stamped on Scuba cylinders provide vital information to those who use and service them.

It is vital to select the right volume Scuba tank for your needs as different sizes are made for different uses.

CARE AND HANDLING OF CYLINDERS

• Never exceed the maximum allowable working pressure.

• Do not allow moisture to enter.

• Store in a cool, dry place with a small amount of pressure in them.

• Fill cylinders slowly.

• Ensure that cylinders are visually inspected and hydrostatically tested in accordance with the country's statutory requirements.

• Do not drain cylinders completely, except for visual inspection.

• Rinse the outside of the cylinder with clean water immediately after use in sea water.

• Do not use dented, welded or scarred cylinders.

• Keep cylinders away from sources of strong heat.

• When transporting cylinders make sure that they are well secured in order to prevent them from rolling about and that the valve is protected from damage at all times.

• Do not drop a cylinder and ensure, therefore, that you have a firm grip before picking it up.

• Do not roll the cylinder or use it as a roller.

• Do not use it to hammer anything.

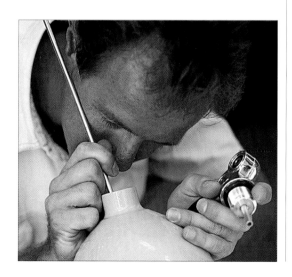

▶ *Annual internal inspection of cylinders is mandatory.*

THE SCUBA AIR-SUPPLY SYSTEM

A Scuba diver's air-supply system consists of a diving cylinder, or tank, in which compressed air is stored; and an on-off cylinder valve situated at the top onto which a two-stage air regulatory system is attached controlling the flow of air. The Scuba air-supply system is simple yet remarkable since it is able to deliver air on demand, from a source of air that is highly compressed, at the ambient pressure exerted upon the diver at different depths. It also, importantly allows the diver complete freedom from the constraints imposed by surface-supplied air systems.

Scuba Cylinders

Scuba cylinders, or tanks, allow the diver to have his or her own source of air. The tank is a cylindrical container made from either steel or aluminium and is available in a variety of sizes and pressure ratings. Twin-cylinder units were once quite popular, but today single tank systems are the most common.

Cylinders are coded and stamped on the shoulder of the tank. The first code is the regulatory agency code which varies from country to country. This may be followed by the metal alloy code – 3AA or 3A denoting steel alloys and 3AL for aluminium alloys. The next code is the maximum working pressure the tank can be pumped to.

Following these codes, usually on the line beneath the regulatory agency code, metal code and working pressure, is the serial number of the cylinder. This number should be recorded and stored in a safe place in order to support identification in the event of the cylinder being stolen or lost. Very important is the test date code; this must contain the month, a special hydro facility mark and the year of the test. Tanks are required to be regularly hydrostatically tested and the tank must be stamped accordingly with the date and testing agent's seal.

It is essential to take good care of diving cylinders. Besides seeing that they are not banged about,

tank coding

dropped or overheated, it is very important to see that moisture does not enter the cylinder. This will combine with high-pressure oxygen to cause insidious corrosion which in due course will weaken the cylinder's metal walls.

Care must be taken of the cylinder during storage. Should there be any moisture in the tank the oxidization process could, over a long period, consume all the oxygen in the air leaving only nitrogen. An unsuspecting diver using the tank will rapidly lose consciousness without warning. Cylinders should thus be stored with only a small amount of air in them and then specifically filled just before use. Before filling, test to see if a whitish mist can be seen when the valve is opened, if water can be heard when the cylinder is tipped back and forth, or if the air has a damp feel or musty smell. Should the cylinder display any of these warning signs do not use it and have it inspected at once. If a cylinder is

emptied completely underwater, it must be visually inspected before being refilled in case the ambient pressure has forced water into it.

All Scuba cylinders must be visually inspected both externally and internally at least once a year by a qualified technician using a special light. If any sign of corrosion is detected it has to be removed. At least once every five years or sooner if required by law, the cylinder must be pressure-tested hydrostatically. This usually involves filling the cylinder with water, placing it in a water-filled pressure chamber and then raising the pressure inside the cylinder using a hydraulic pump. The expansion of the cylinder is measured by the amount of water displaced in the water column. The pressure is increased to five-thirds of the rated pressure of the cylinder and a permanent expansion of 10% or more of the total expansion will render the cylinder unsafe and unfit for further use. It will thus be condemned.

▲ *Scuba offers the diver total freedom of movement.*

WAYS FOR WATER TO ENTER A CYLINDER

• The presence of water on the cylinder valve or on the compressor filler attachment at the time of filling.

• Drawing air from a cylinder underwater to such an extent that the pressure in the tank is lower than the ambient pressure. This results in back flow through the regulator and the entry of water into the cylinder.

• Leaving the valve open, thus causing a rapid change in temperature and heavy condensation.

• A defective or improperly operated compressor.

CYLINDER VALVES AND ASSEMBLIES

A Scuba cylinder valve is a simple on-off valve that controls high-pressure gas manually. Today the K-valve has become the standard cylinder valve in recreation diving as it is simple and reliable.

Cylinder valves incorporate a burst disc device which is a built-in safety feature designed to prevent the cylinder pressure reaching dangerously high levels due to a lack of caution during filling or under conditions of extreme heat (e.g. fire).

Burst discs are rated at five-thirds of the working pressure of the cylinder; should this pressure be exceeded, the disc will burst with a loud bang and hiss of air, but no damage will be done – other than to your frayed nerves! Without this safety device the cylinder would turn into a potential bomb which could cause considerable damage should its specifications be exceeded.

Cylinder valves are important items of Scuba equipment; correct usage and maintenance are vital. Excessive force should never be used when turning a Scuba valve on or off as valve seat discs, gaskets or 'o' ring seals can be easily damaged. Valves should always be turned slowly and gently until fully opened; it is then advisable to close the valve one-quarter turn in order to reduce the pressure on the stem seal. Cylinder valves should be serviced annually to reduce the possibility of valve seizure.

The K-valve is a simple on-off valve situated at the top of the cylinder.

▶ *For safe, enjoyable diving, it is vital that your equipment is in excellent condition.*

K-VALVE MECHANISM

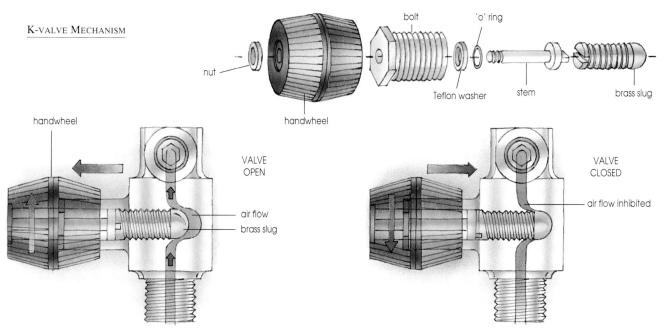

nut · handwheel · bolt · 'o' ring · Teflon washer · stem · brass slug · handwheel

handwheel · VALVE OPEN · air flow · brass slug

handwheel · VALVE CLOSED · air flow inhibited

to an intermediate pressure of between 7–10 bar (90–130psi) above ambient pressure and the **second stage** then further reduces the intermediate air pressure to ambient pressure.

SINGLE-HOSE REGULATOR

There are technically two types of regulator: twin-hose and single-hose. **Twin-hose** regulators were the original ones used in Scuba diving and combined both stages into one mechanical assembly mounted onto the cylinder valve. Two flexible hoses lead from either side of the assembly to a mouthpiece containing both inhalation and exhalation nonreturn valves – the hose that passes over the right shoulder carries fresh air from the cylinder and the hose over the left shoulder carries exhaled air that is exhausted into the water through the regulator assembly on the cylinder. Twin-hose regulators are favoured by some underwater photographers as the expelled air rises behind the head and not in front of the face or camera.

- hose connector to BC
- instrument console
- mouthpiece and second stage
- back-up mouthpiece
- first stage

SCUBA REGULATORS

The function of a Scuba regulator is to reduce the high pressure contained in the Scuba cylinder to a usable level and to deliver this air only on demand. Regulators make use of the pressure differential created by the respiratory action of the diver's lungs to regulate air flow between the cylinder and the lungs, automatically adjusting to changes in depth and the diver's respiration rate.

This ability to reduce the pressure of air in the cylinder to ambient (i.e. surrounding pressure) and to deliver the air on demand to the diver is achieved in two stages. The **first stage** reduces cylinder pressure from between 200–344 bar (2000–3000psi)

TWIN-HOSE REGULATOR

Single-hose regulators are the standard type of regulator in use today because they are reliable, simple, highly efficient and easy to maintain. With a single-hose regulator the first stage of pressure reduction is attached to the cylinder valve, while the second stage and exhaust port are incorporated into the mouthpiece assembly. The two stages are connected by a single intermediate pressure hose.

Other hoses may also be incorporated into the single-hose regulator system. These can include hoses connected to the buoyancy compensator, a back-up 'octopus' rig, an instrument console and even air-powered tools.

Regulators are designed to accommodate a number of attachments:

- A submersible pressure gauge (SPG) which is connected to the first stage by means of a single high-pressure hose.
- A buoyancy compensator (BC) inflator low-pressure hose which is connected between the first stage and the inlet port on the BC.
  - An 'octopus' rig, which is an extra second stage that is used as a back-up in the event of equipment failure or for buddy-breathing.
    - A dry-suit inflator hose.

The second stage reduces the intermediate pressure to that needed for respiration.

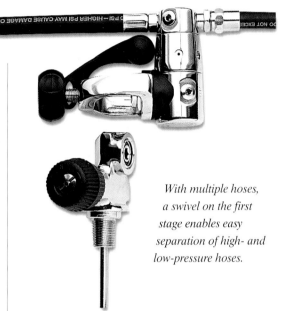

With multiple hoses, a swivel on the first stage enables easy separation of high- and low-pressure hoses.

Regular care and maintenance of regulators is essential. They must be carefully washed after every dive – soaking in warmish fresh water and rinsing afterwards is advised. The first-stage dust cover should be in place at all times when the regulator is not in use.

Regulators should not be lubricated and silicone spray should be avoided as it can be detrimental to the diaphragm and other parts of the regulator. The regulator should be functionally tested every six months and serviced annually.

It is important to keep a watchful eye on the coloration of the external filter on the first stage of the regulator since it will give some indication of the condition of the cylinder you are using. A greenish filter either indicates corrosion in the cylinder or the presence of water in the first stage; a reddish filter indicates rust from a steel cylinder; and a deep grey or blackish filter will indicate carbon dust in the

THE OPERATION OF THE DEMAND VALVE

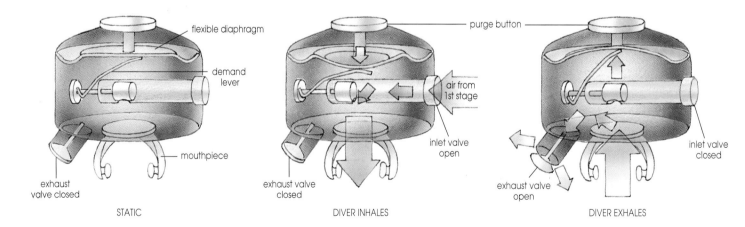

STATIC

DIVER INHALES

DIVER EXHALES

A diaphragm is fitted over an open dish-like chamber which contains an inlet valve, an exhaust valve and an opening to the mouthpiece. The inlet valve is coupled to the diaphragm in such a way that when the diver inhales, the diaphragm is pushed in by the ambient water pressure to the point where the tilt valve allows air into the mouthpiece. When the diver stops inhaling air pressure inside the chamber forces the diaphragm outward and, when the internal pressure equals the ambient pressure, the valve closes and allows no more air in. This ability to balance pressure enables the regulator to operate at any depth. The exhaust valve remains closed until the diver exhales into the regulator; this creates an internal pressure that forces the exhaust valve open and the exhaled air escapes into the water.

cylinder usually as a result of a defective compressor filter. The indicated problems should be attended to professionally. While underwater you should have your buddy check your first stage for small bubbles which will indicate the presence of a leak – most divemasters will permit the completion of the dive if the leak is very small, but the problem must be attended to before the next dive. You should likewise check the second stage for leaks. It is important to protect all the hoses of your regulator; a good idea is to have **rubber sleeves**, **strain reliefs** or **hose protectors**, fitted over them.

While on the beach, either preparing to dive or after a dive, great care must be taken to see that the regulator is kept away from the sand as a single grain could lodge in the demand valve and cause it to jam underwater. To remedy this situation connect the regulator to a cylinder, pressurize it and then submerge it in water, moving it rapidly back and forth while purging the second stage. This should dislodge any grains of sand stuck in the demand valve. Should you have any doubts, have the regulator checked out professionally before using it again. Avoid pulling on the hoses while handling your equipment as this could weaken them.

SUBMERSIBLE PRESSURE GAUGES (SPGS)

Submersible pressure gauges are attached to the high-pressure port of the first stage of the regulator and provide a continual read-out of the air pressure in the cylinder. Most SPGs are based on a spiral form of the Bourdon movement gauge. This is a flattened helix tube, sealed at one end. As the spiral is pressurized it uncoils because of pressure differences between the inner and outer arcs of the spiral tubing. The closed end of the tube is attached to a lever system that moves an indicator needle in accordance with the pressure levels in the cylinder.

New digital pressure gauges are beginning to gain ground in the marketplace. Some use a pressure-sensitive transductor that transmits a signal from a unit mounted on the cylinder valve to a battery-powered electronically driven liquid-crystal display gauge fitted into the diver's instrument console.

An SPG is **not** an optional accessory! The diver must know at all times how much air is in the tank

thus ensuring that there is sufficient reserve to meet any emergencies that may arise. An SPG should be purchased at the same time as the regulator.

Although it is a delicate instrument, an SPG requires no special maintenance other than normal washing. However, it is important while opening your cylinder valve **not** to look closely at your SPG, since if there is a leak in the gauge's Bourdon movement, air will flow into the gauge housing; this could cause it to explode in your face should the safety plug malfunction. Avoid obstructing the area over the plug so that it is free to blow out and release pressure if necessary. Should water be present inside your SPG, have it serviced immediately and do not use it until you have done so.

The pressure gauge is a vital control instrument in diving.

▶ *Buddies should check each other's gear before diving.*

CAPILLARY GAUGE

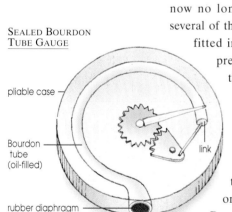

water

air bubble

OPEN BOURDON TUBE GAUGE

Bourdon tube

rigid case

link

inlet and filter

SEALED BOURDON TUBE GAUGE

pliable case

Bourdon tube (oil-filled)

link

rubber diaphragm

DIAPHRAGM GAUGE

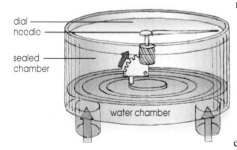

dial

needle

sealed chamber

water chamber

DEPTH GAUGES

There are a number of types of depth gauge available, each using a different method for recording depth. The simplest and least expensive is the **capillary gauge**. This comprises a circular tube sealed at one end. As water enters the tube, the air is compressed proportionately to depth, according to Boyle's Law. The scale against which the capillary tube is set is nonlinear, and therefore the graduations on the scale become difficult to read in deeper water and at low light levels. There are also problems associated with clogging and the presence of air bubbles in the tube, thus a capillary-based depth gauge should not be used as a primary instrument.

One advantage of capillary depth gauges, however, is in altitude diving where they automatically provide equivalent depth readings at higher elevations. They are also accurate at shallow depths thus making them ideal for decompression/safety stops.

The **open Bourdon tube** depth gauge, now no longer available, forms the basis for several of the gauges currently in use. The tube is fitted inside a housing and as water enters, pressure is exerted on the entrapped air thus driving the Bourdon movement.

The **sealed Bourdon tube** depth gauge is an advance on the open Bourdon tube as the tube is sealed and fluid-filled, preventing corrosion and silting. At the one end is a diaphragm through which pressure is exerted on the fluid and this, as with the open Bourdon tube, activates the instrument.

The **diaphragm depth gauge** is a mechanical depth gauge which does not use the Bourdon movement; instead a gearing mechanism linked to an indicator needle is activated by water pressure exerted on a thin metal diaphragm mounted in a rigid, hermetically sealed case.

These gauges can be adjusted to give accurate readings at altitude, however they are generally more expensive than the Bourdon gauges.

Digital depth gauges are electronically operated and are similar to electronic cylinder pressure gauges, except for the fact that they operate at lower pressures. These gauges are extremely accurate and can incorporate other features, such as a maximum depth indicator and an ascent-rate indicator. However, they are sensitive to temperature variations, require batteries to operate, and can be difficult to read in poor lighting conditions unless the instrument has a backlit screen. They are also vulnerable to damage if exposed to reduced pressures when flying and should therefore only be transported in a tightly sealed container or pressurized aircraft cabin.

There are several types of analogue gauge.

An important feature in a depth gauge is a maximum depth indicator which is mechanically operated in analogue gauges and electronically operated in digital ones. Maximum depth reached on a dive is an important factor in calculating bottom time and the length of time required for decompression stops.

UNDERWATER WATCHES

Underwater watches, or timers, are available in both analogue and digital format. An analogue dive watch usually has a rotating collar, or bezel, which can be aligned with the minute hand at the start of the dive, thus fixing the start time. The difference between this and the time at the end of the dive indicates the time elapsed, that is, the length of the dive. Digital watches are popular among many divers as they offer features such as a stopwatch, timer, alarm and screen light. Dive watches should be well rinsed after every dive and it is important not to wear them in hot baths or showers as high temperatures and soap are detrimental.

An underwater watch is a necessity.

ELECTRONIC DIVE COMPUTERS

Electronic dive computers only activate upon submersion. They include some or all of the following:
- Present depth indicator
- Maximum depth reached on the dive
- Elapsed bottom time
- No-decompression-time remaining
- Dive time remaining, based on air supply and consumption
- Air pressure
- Water temperature
- Surface interval required before diving again
- Ascent rate
- Decompression stop depth
- Decompression time required
- Scrolling, which displays the no-decompression limits for various depths for repetitive dives
- Time to wait before flying
- Battery level
- Dive number
- Dive profile

There are two types of decompression computers, the one, tissue-based and the other, table-based. Tissue-based computers continuously calculate nitrogen absorption against theoretical tissue models, while table-based dive computers compare time and depth data with mathematical models based on appropriate dive tables. Because these calculations are continuous they compensate for the time spent at various depths throughout the dive and these continuous multilevel calculations usually allow for a longer bottom time than would normally be permissible with 'square' dive profiles. The latter are based on dive tables which are calculated on the total time allowed at the maximum depth reached during the dive; they are, therefore, inevitably more restrictive. Decompression computers will display a warning when the no-decompression limit is being approached or exceeded – in which case decompression depths and time requirements will be displayed.

It is important to note that all computer calculations are based on the physical strength and fitness of the average diver and on normal diving conditions. Some models may take into account the relative warmth or coolness of the water, but the computer has no way of knowing your age, whether you are feeling tired and whether you have to exert yourself against strong prevailing currents or surge.

There are some computer models which will allow the diver to make adjustments in order to take most of these factors into account but it is important for divers to adjust and limit their own dive profiles accordingly. Also, computers are not infallible and are subject to operational failure. Divers should, therefore, carry a back-up depth gauge and underwater watch plus a set of dive tables in case the computer should fail. In this eventuality the dive should be aborted and a decompression stop made for safety's sake. Dive buddies should not share one computer, particularly if they are planning a no-decompression dive as no two dive profiles are ever exactly the same.

Dive computers are sensitive instruments and should be carefully looked after. Shock, exposure to heat and close proximity to strong magnetic fields should be avoided. After each dive they should be thoroughly rinsed and a careful check kept on battery power.

Computers take the hassle out of diving, but they are fallible.

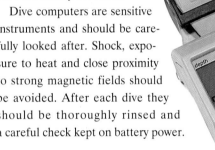

DIVING COMPASS

Diving compasses, either dry or liquid-filled, are extremely useful instruments, particularly on low visibility and special-assignment diving. Liquid-filled compasses consist of a magnetic disc or arrow, known as a **compass card,** which rests on a bearing. The card is partially supported by the liquid in order to reduce the load on the bearing and to dampen the movement of the compass card, making it easier to read. These compasses are unaffected by pressure.

Dry compasses are similar to liquid-filled compasses except that the compass card does not have a float assembly and this, as well as the absence of liquid, makes it a lot lighter. However, the compass card tends to oscillate more, while the compass is subject to the effects of pressure and is more unreliable.

Compasses are precision instruments and should be properly cared for and maintained. They should not be exposed to heat and hot sunlight for any length of time.

For quick reference and ease of carrying, instruments are put into a console which is attached to the high-pressure hose mounted on the first stage.

EXPOSURE SUITS

The essential task of an exposure suit is to prevent excessive loss of body heat, while a supplementary task is to provide protection from some of the sea's stings and scrapes. Since diving involves being in water for prolonged periods, exposure suits are of value in almost all conditions – even in warm tropical seas. However, the type of suit and thickness of material vary according to conditions.

▶ *The one-piece suit prevents water from entering around the diver's middle, but can be difficult to get into and out of.*

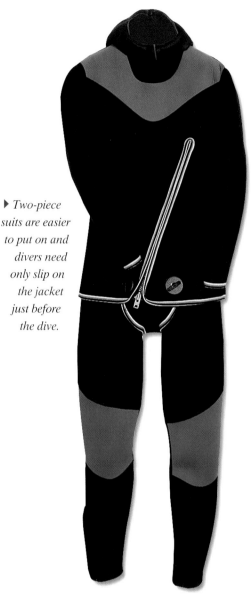

▶ *Two-piece suits are easier to put on and divers need only slip on the jacket just before the dive.*

▲ *Three-quarter-length wet suits can be used on their own or with long johns beneath.*

WET SUITS

One of the most common types of exposure suit used in recreational diving is the **wet suit**. Made from closed-cell neoprene, it is designed to fit the body tightly but comfortably in order to minimize the amount of water entering between the suit and the diver's body. This water is soon heated by the diver's body and this helps to provide insulation against cold external water temperatures. If the suit does not fit tightly enough water will circulate and the constant inflow of fresh cold water will reduce the effectiveness of the wet suit.

Suits come in various thicknesses in order to provide variable insulation against different water temperatures – a tropical wet suit would not be suitable for temperate waters and vice versa!

Since wet suits are made from a material that is composed of thousands of tiny air cells, it is buoyant; the diver must therefore carry weights in order to get below the surface. After the dive it is essential that the wet suit is thoroughly washed – both inside and out – in order to remove any sea water absorbed by the neoprene material. It should then be hung up on a padded coathanger in a cool, well-aired room well out of the sun's heat, since neoprene will perish if exposed for any length of time to direct sunlight.

Continuing to gain in popularity is the **Lycra** or **sea skin suit**. This is made from a stretch Lycra and is commonly used in warmer waters. It offers minimal resistance to cold, but does provide protection from stings and exposure to the sun.

▶ *Compressed neoprene suits possess the ability to stretch and can thus follow the contours of the diver's body.*

◀ *Vulcanized rubber has traditionally been used for most dry suits. It is strong and durable.*

DRY SUITS

Dry suits are made from a variety of waterproof materials such as vulcanized rubber, waterproofed nylons and compressed neoprene. Most suits are designed to seal around the wrists and neck, and are equipped with waterproof zippers. Dry suits have a low-pressure inflator mechanism which is connected to a low-pressure port in the regulator's first stage. This is used to inflate the interior of the suit, thus preventing suit squeeze at depth and providing buoyancy. The suit has exhaust valves, often located on the sleeves, allowing air to escape on ascent.

The purpose of the dry suit is to provide a waterproof, protective 'outer skin' under which the diver is able to wear warm underclothing. Furthermore, the air that is trapped within the dry suit steadily warms up through body heat and this also helps to insulate the diver against the surrounding cold water. It is important that dry-suit underwear does not compress drastically under pressure since, if it does, it will not work efficiently at depth.

Care must be taken not to wear garments which give off fibres since these may clog the dry suit exhaust valve thus hampering its efficiency or worse still, jamming it open or closed.

If the exhaust valve is jammed open, it will leak and cause the diver to get wet with a probably serious loss of body heat; if it jams closed, it will prevent the diver from venting air and this could cause the diver to have an uncontrolled ascent with potentially harmful consequences.

▲ *Dry suit undergarments help to provide insulation for the diver and should thus be chosen with care.*

DIVING HOODS, BOOTIES AND GLOVES

These items of diving equipment prevent heat loss at the extremities as well as providing protection against cuts, abrasions and stings from contact with rocks, corals and other elements in the sea. An uncovered head is a major source of heat loss, therefore wearing a hood in cold water is essential.

WEIGHT BELTS

Exposure suits and Scuba gear result in divers becoming positively buoyant. In order to counteract this, it is necessary for the diver to wear a weight belt so that neutral buoyancy can be achieved. Lead weights come in various shapes and styles and are attached to a belt that is worn around the diver's waist. The number of weights is dependent upon the diver's physiology and their configuration is a matter of personal preference. It is vital that the weight belt has a quick-release buckle so that it may be jettisoned easily in an emergency.

DIVING KNIVES

A diving knife is an important part of the diver's equipment. It is used for cutting, prying, digging, measuring and, very importantly, for knocking against the diving cylinder in order to attract the attention of other divers in an emergency situation or for simple communication. The blade of the knife should have a sharp cutting edge on one side and a serrated edge on the other in order to facilitate sawing through rope, seaweed or fishing lines – all of which could entangle the diver under water.

Quick access to the knife is important and it should be kept in a quick-release sheath strapped in an easily accessible place – most divers tend to prefer the inner leg below the knee as this lessens the chances of the knife catching on anything.

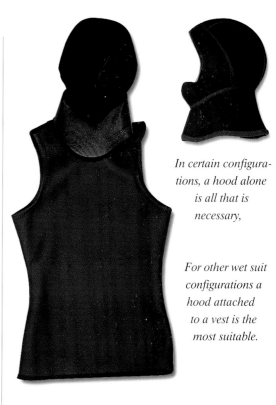

In certain configurations, a hood alone is all that is necessary,

For other wet suit configurations a hood attached to a vest is the most suitable.

AIR COMPRESSORS

Two types of compressors are available depending on the form of diving being undertaken. For Scuba diving, high-pressure, low-volume compressors are needed to fill the diver's cylinder, while for industrial diving, where the diver's air is supplied through an umbilical hose from the surface, a low-pressure, high-volume compressor is required.

Care must be taken to ensure that all lubricants are nontoxic and the air inlet is kept well free from possible contamination.

Compressors are based on the principle of Boyle's Law – pressure is increased by reducing volume. Air is compressed in stages, with the volume of the compression cylinder decreasing in each stage so that the pressure is steadily built up. Nonreturn valves ensure that compressed air is prevented from returning to a previous stage.

Air compressors are driven by either internal combustion or electric motors. Electric motors are preferable since they are convenient and fewer toxins are generated; however, in those areas where electricity is not available, such as at remote dive locations, it is necessary to use compressors driven by internal combustion engines.

The choice of glove depends on whether the major consideration is warmth or protection.

▶ *Knives are usually worn on the inside of the leg for ease of access.*

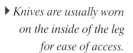

Booties are used with open-heel fins; they prevent heat loss in cold water and protect the diver's feet.

◀▼ Marker buoys are essential on drift dives.

◀ For their own safety, divers should be properly equipped at all times.

When air is compressed it becomes heated and its moisture content rises in relation to volume. As a high moisture content is undesirable in Scuba cylinders, it must be removed. The air is passed through an expansion chamber causing it to cool and the moisture to condense into water, which collects at the bottom; this is then periodically drained off. The dry compressed air is fed to a storage tank, called an **air bank**, from where compressed air is drawn off through a manifold system in order to simultaneously fill a number of Scuba cylinders as and when required. Portable compressors are useful for diving in remote locations.

It is important to ensure that all air filters are clean and well maintained and that the air inlet is far removed from any pollutant source such as the compressor engine's exhaust.

Weight belts counter a diver's positive buoyancy.

CHAPTER FOUR

TRAINING

Formal training in Scuba diving and the success-ful completion of a training course accredited to an internationally recognized diving association is necessary for any diver who is serious about the sport and who wishes to participate in an organized way. Diving is undeniably dangerous; however, the risks can be vastly reduced through proper training and conscientious observance of sound diving practice. While it may be possible in some sports to do away with formal instruction and to acquire the necessary skills through practice and experimen-tation, this is not the case with diving – a single mishap underwater could cost the diver his or her life. Training also provides knowledge; this brings confidence which, in turn, enhances enjoyment.

Finally, without accredited recognition of an acceptable diving qualification, no diver will be allowed to dive at any reputable diving centre anywhere in the world. Thus, a 'C-card' or equivalent, on which your qualifications are recorded, is your passport to diving happiness.

DIVING ORGANIZATIONS

Diving training is formally organized under the auspices of a number of international diving asso-ciations responsible for establishing and maintaining standards of diving instruction, training accredita-tion and certification. The following are some of the most prominent international associations:

The **British Sub Aqua Club** (BSAC) was formed in London in 1953 by a group of divers who came together 'to promote underwater exploration, sci-ence and safety in these activities'. By the end of 1954 the Club was officially recognized in Britain as the governing body for 'the new sport of underwater swimming'. In 1959, BSAC became a founding

Come here.

An exciting world filled with unusual experiences opens up to the trained diver.

member of Confédération Mondiale des Activités Subaquatiques (CMAS), the World Underwater Federation. By 1976, diving had become such a popular sport in the United Kingdom that the Club decided to establish the BSAC School system. These are independent businesses which are authorized to train and award a number of BSAC diving qualifications. Today there are over 200 schools throughout the world and BSAC has established a network of branches internationally.

The Scottish Sub Aqua Club (SSAC), formed in 1951, is actually the oldest known diving organization but only has approximately 5000 members. Training is almost identical to that of the BSAC.

Watch me.

▲ *Buddies must keep together and in contact with the rest of the group.*

The **Confédération Mondiale des Activités Subaquatiques** (CMAS), was created in 1959 in Monaco to unite all the national diving organizations that were beginning to develop worldwide. Its first president was the famous underwater explorer Jacques-Yves Cousteau. Over 90 national diving federations, unions and associations and 50 scientific, educational and affiliated organizations are members of CMAS. Every year over 100,000 certificates are issued to divers who have qualified through a course conducted under the federation's auspices. CMAS, whose headquarters are in Rome, is a member of several international organizations including:

• United Nations Educational, Scientific and Cultural Organization (UNESCO)
• International Olympic Committee (IOC)
• World Wide Fund for Nature (WWF).

CMAS-registered training is officially recognized worldwide by many governmental and statutory bodies and large companies as the required underwater training qualification for employment.

CMAS is also involved in all aspects of underwater activity. Its objectives are to support research, to further technical development in diving, to promote safety, and to supervise the organization of underwater sports activities. This work is done under the direction and control of three separate committees: sports, technical and scientific.

The **Professional Association of Diving Instructors** (PADI) is based in Santa Ana, California, and is presently considered to be the largest diver-training organization. It provides training materials and support to some 60,000 professional members who offer diving instruction at 3000 PADI Dive Centres and Resorts situated throughout the world. PADI promotes an Action Plan which is a system of diver education designed to take the student step-by-step through a variety of courses, each backed by books, videos and other support materials. Through PADI Dive Centres and Resorts, practical training is provided so that students can apply the diving principles learnt. These centres also hire out and sell equipment as well as offer general customer service.

The **National Association of Underwater Instructors** (NAUI) is based at Montclair, California, and is the largest democratic, nonprofit diving instructor membership organization in the world. Similarly to PADI, NAUI offers a diving training certification programme for use by professional diving instructors. It is owned and operated as a nonprofit association by its voting membership and is managed by a board of directors voted in annually by all paid-up members. Through this democratic process, NAUI is able to represent the voice of its members. The association provides support services, course development assistance and quality control to its members through staff located at NAUI headquarters. In addition, NAUI's marketing department also supports its members through the promotion of diving and diver education in both national and international media.

TRAINING QUALIFICATIONS

Diving training is a progressive, didactic process with the student passing through a series of grades. The Novice or Basic Scuba course is designed to provide the aspirant diver with the essential knowledge and skills needed for open water diving. This is then followed by a structured programme of diving courses, all of which embrace both theoretical instruction and practical application, and which enable the student to graduate to higher levels of competence and diving specialization.

With each level, the diver obtains not only internationally accepted accreditation, but also more knowledge of the underwater world and new and different ways of enjoying it. This graded learning process enables trainees to develop knowledge through experience and safety awareness through sound technique.

DIVE QUALIFICATIONS

Various diving associations have different titles for essentially equivalent levels of diving. In this book the following titles will be used for the different levels of training:

Snorkel Diver: a short course to introduce trainees to the underwater world and to create confidence.

Basic Scuba Diver: a short course given in a swimming pool designed to introduce the novice to diving; also known as a Resort Diving Course as many dive centres are based at resort hotels throughout the world.

Open Water Diver: the first level of open water Scuba diving.

Advanced Open Water Diver: further consolidation and intensification of the knowledge and skills learnt in the Open Water course.

Master Diver: the highest nonleadership grade; a qualification given to divers of many years' standing who have appropriate experience and diving expertise.

Divemaster and **Assistant Instructor**: the first levels of diving leadership further developing the knowledge and skills of the diver as well as providing training in leadership skills so that the trainee is fully competent to lead a dive group.

Diving Instructor: this qualification enables the diver to teach, which for many becomes a professional or part-time occupation.

Master Instructor: the highest level of instruction presently available.

◀ *In clear water it is easier to maintain visual contact.*

SNORKEL DIVER TRAINING

Scuba training usually commences with a course in snorkelling as this is the logical intermediate stage between ordinary swimming and Scuba diving. Snorkelling increases physical fitness, swimming ability, confidence and general water discipline. It also exposes the aspirant diver to the effects of water pressure and to some of the problems and require-ments of diving such as: ear-clearing, equalizing mask pressure, differences in vision due to refrac-tion, underwater signalling and how to use a snorkel, mask and fins. In addition, training in essential safety rules is given during the course.

BASIC SCUBA COURSE

Once the trainer is satisfied that the pupil has completed his or her snorkel proficiency test, the Basic Scuba Diving Course begins. Initial training is conducted in a swimming pool or in very sheltered waters. The purpose of this course is to familiarize the pupil with all aspects of Scuba diving equipment.

Instruction commences with a lecture on the basics of diving and the use of Scuba equipment. After this, the instructor demonstrates the prepara-tion of diving equipment and pre-dive checks, using his own set. The students then follow, preparing and checking their own equipment under the supervision of the diving instructor. Once satisfied that everyone is comfortable, the instructor and students enter the training pool and practise breathing underwater. This is a time when the novice can learn in complete safety and gain confidence. It is important for pupils to surface at regular intervals and to discuss any problems or difficulties they may have with the instructor. All nagging doubts or feelings of uncer-tainty should be ironed out at this early stage.

Once the trainer is satisfied that his or her pupils are ready the first dive is undertaken. This is nor-mally a shallow dive (less than 10m; 30ft) done in calm conditions. Basic Scuba courses are not always certification courses but rather orientation courses. Their purpose is to give a person a taste of diving and the beauty of the underwater world. They are designed to provide two open water dives and lim-ited training in problem management.

◀ *Even with snorkelling, buoyancy control is vital because of the risk of damaging delicate reefs.*

OPEN WATER ONE TRAINING

Open Water One training is a basic course in which trainees are taken to a level of competency which permits diving to a maximum depth of 18m (60ft). The training curriculum for most associations consists of five academic sessions, five skills-development sessions, an open-water skin dive, and four or five open-water Scuba dives.

In order to take the course, the aspirant diver must be able to demonstrate certain basic water skills without using swimming aids.

The first theoretical module of the Open Water training programme deals with the basic physics of diving. Its purpose is to enable divers to understand the factors affecting the buoyancy of an object; to explain pressure, volume and density relationships; their effects on the diver; and how to prevent discomfort or injury due to pressure changes.

The second theoretical module deals with equipment. Its purpose is to explain the function of each item of equipment; the different types that are used in diving and their main features; and how to use, care for and maintain them. The items of equipment that are covered in this module include masks, snorkels, fins, buoyancy control devices, tanks, valves, regulators and backpacks.

In the skills-development session pupils receive instruction in:

• Preparing, dressing and adjusting equipment ready for diving

• Using a BC on the surface (and then practising in water too deep to stand)

• Recovering a regulator hose from behind the diver's shoulder

• Clearing a regulator of water using the exhalation and purge clearing methods

• Clearing a partially flooded mask underwater

• Finning underwater without any arm movement

• Ascending and descending with Scuba equipment

• Removing a regulator from a Scuba tank correctly.

The next module deals with some of the major characteristics of the underwater environment and how it differs from the terrestrial environment. At the end of this module, pupils must be able to explain the differences in vision, hearing, heat loss and body movements in the two environments.

The following module deals with respiration underwater; here breathing efficiency while diving as well as what to do to prevent choking on inhaled water is explained. How to cope with overexertion is also dealt with in the course.

Diving instruments and how to use them is sometimes given as a separate module at this juncture in certain training programmes, if it has not already been dealt with as part of the equipment training module given earlier.

The purpose is to explain the need for a **watch** and its importance in calculating bottom time; the use of a **depth gauge** and the need to be aware of depth at all times; using a diving **compass** underwater; how to use a dive **computer** and the importance of keeping a regular check on tank pressure by regularly monitoring the **SPG**.

Having reference information at all times during the dive is essential as this helps the diver to plan, make correct decisions and dive safely.

▲ *Checking one's equipment before a dive is essential.*

REQUIREMENTS FOR OPEN WATER ONE

1. Swimming a minimum of 180m (200yd) nonstop using two or more swimming strokes.
2. Swimming 12m (40ft) underwater on a single breath of air.
3. Diving down 3–4m (10–13ft), recovering a 2.5kg (5.5lb) object, and bringing it to the surface.
4. Treading water for five minutes.
5. Floating unaided and with minimum movement for five minutes.

HAND SIGNALS

Communications are important underwater and in order to avoid confusion, internationally recognized diving signals have been devised with which all divers must be thoroughly conversant. This is one of the most important modules in Open Water One training.

O.K?/O.K.

O.K?/O.K.
(one hand occupied)

O.K?/O.K.
(on surface at a distance)

O.K?/O.K.

Stop/hold it/stay there

Something is wrong

Me/watch me

Come here

Go down/going down

Go that way

Go up/going up

Level off at this depth

Low on air

Low on air
(alternate version)

Which direction?

Buddy breathe/share air

Buddy breathe/share air
(alternate version)

Hold hands

Out of air

Take it easy/slow down

You lead, I'll follow

Get with your buddy

Ears not clearing

Ears not clearing
(alternate version)

Distress/Help

I am cold

Danger

HOW TO ENTER THE WATER IN DIFFERENT DIVE LOCATIONS

An important module in the Open Water training programme involves instruction on how to enter the water in different dive locations while fully kitted up. If it is a shore, river or lake dive and you can wade into the water or lower yourself in by using a ladder or similar means, no special technique is required.

If you are diving from a boat or entering the water from a height, entry technique becomes important. In the case of entry from a boat the procedure most frequently used is to sit on the gunwale of the boat with your back to the water and with your feet in the boat (ensuring that your fins are free and will be unrestricted by fittings and other impediments when your feet lift out of the boat). Then, holding your mask securely against your face with one hand and your regulator in your mouth with the other, roll backwards into the water. It should be noted that although backward entry is probably the most common method of entry from smaller boats, it is not necessarily the best method. An alternative (slower) method is to place both legs over the side of the boat and twist around while holding on to the gunwale to slip gently into the water.

Once in the water you should immediately clear the area to make space for other divers to follow you and also to distance yourself from the boat in case it should hit you as it rides the sea's swell.

SUMMARY OF ENTRY PROCEDURES

1. Make sure the entry area is clear of all forms of obstruction.
2. With shore dives, partially inflate the BC to provide instant buoyancy.
3. Make sure your buddy is fully kitted up and ready to enter.
4. Follow the entry procedure required by the boat skipper if you are diving from a boat, or according to the dive plan agreed upon prior to the dive.
5. Hold your face mask and regulator firmly in place if there is a possibility of them becoming dislodged.
6. Immediately after entering the water, clear the area and wait a safe distance away for your buddy; then descend.
7. Rendezvous at the bottom with the rest of the dive party, according to the dive plan.

Should your entry point be high up, you could jump in a stride position with one foot behind the other. On impact with the surface, draw your legs together so that you will not penetrate too deeply into the water. The safer method is to lower yourself into the water, as described above. Buddies should try to enter the water together and then descend as soon they can to the prearranged meeting point at the bottom. The sea's surface is a dangerous place, so divers should linger there as little as possible.

THE BUDDY SYSTEM

The importance of the buddy system cannot be overestimated. Diving is not a loner sport; every diver must have a buddy and they should dive together. The main reason for this is safety, since buddies are required to keep a constant watch on one another and be on hand to assist or to call for assistance in the event of an emergency. A buddy can also generally assist in kitting up, checking on equipment (left) and simply sharing underwater experiences. Before entering the water, buddies should face each other and check to see that:

• The BC is properly adjusted and the tank properly secured
• The BC is fully functional, with both the mechanical inflator and oral inflator operating correctly
• The weight belt is properly secured and is over all other gear so that it can be easily dumped in the event of an emergency
• The air supply is turned on, all hoses are clear and untwisted and there is more than sufficient air for the dive
• There are no dangling straps, trapped hoses or missing gear.

Dive planning is essential and should be done as part of the diving teamwork. In this module the instructor is required to elaborate on buddy system procedures, emphasizing that the prime responsibility of a buddy is to prevent problems from happening and secondly, to assist when they do. It is vital that all members of the dive are fully conversant with the dive plan and have a reasonable idea of conditions. There should be agreement on entry and exit points if it is a shore dive, the course of the dive, bottom time, depth and air supply limits, techniques of staying together and the procedure to follow in the event of separation. Buddies should never be more than about 2–3m (6–10ft) apart, should maintain the same position relative to one another and should generally follow one direction. If a change in direction is decided by one partner, this should be conveyed to the other and agreement on the new direction must be acknowledged by both partners. In the event of buddies becoming separated they should first search for one another, but this must be for no longer than a minute after which both should return to the surface and reunite there.

In the Open Water training programme **entry procedures** are practised, as is breathing with a snorkel while fully kitted up and the procedures to be followed in changing from a snorkel to a regulator and vice versa.

Breathing without a mask underwater forms another important part of the training programme, as does mask replacement. It is vital that the diver can carry out these functions without hesitation since a mask could easily be dislodged underwater as a result of the inadvertent sweep of a fellow diver's fin as he or she passes by.

Just as entry procedures are practised so too are **exit procedures**. Obviously with shore dives, where it is possible to walk or clamber out of the water, no special training procedures are required. However, never enter or exit from the water where the sea is

▼ Holding hands is mutually supportive, especially in adverse conditions.

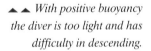

▲▲ With positive buoyancy the diver is too light and has difficulty in descending.

▲ With negative buoyancy the diver is too heavy and tends to sink.

▲ ▶ With neutral buoyancy the diver remains at the same level.

rough, or around rocks as the surge can quite easily harm a diver. Remember that a 2m-high (6ft) wave will have a 2m trough making a combined drop of 4m (13ft). With deep-water diving where a boat is used, the correct procedure for exiting the water must be followed. Firstly, the weight belt should be removed and either fixed to a rope attached to the boat or handed to the skipper or a fellow diver who has exited before you. The mask should then be removed and passed into the boat. The diving tank and BC follow. The last item to be removed are fins as they are useful to help you tread water as well as to propel you upwards when climbing into the boat.

Buoyancy control is an important module. The ideal is for the diver to maintain neutral buoyancy as this means that the diver does not have to expend energy in trying to keep down or off the bottom. In environmentally sensitive dive areas dive centres may refuse to take a diver down who is unable to achieve neutral buoyancy, because of the damage done by divers crashing into fragile coral reefs.

Buoyancy is controlled by three factors: the first is the weight of the diver when kitted up; the second is the amount of air in the BC (and dry suit); and the third is the amount of air in the diver's lungs. The variable weight of the diver is determined by the number of weights carried on the weight belt which should be set at a level sufficient to cause negative buoyancy. To counteract the negative buoyancy the BC is inflated until neutral buoyancy is achieved.

Many diving instructors teach their pupils the basics of neutral buoyancy by requiring them to lie face down on the bottom of a pool while breathing slowly and deeply and then to add air to the BC until the upper part of the body rises slightly, allowing it to pivot upwards on the tips of the diver's fins while inhaling and to pivot downwards on exhalation.

Buoyancy is not constant as a change in depth results in a change in the volume of air in the wet suit (or dry suit) and therefore it is necessary to adjust buoyancy with changes in depth. This is done by either adding air to the BC (or dry suit, which helps to prevent squeeze) or by expelling it, depending on the circumstances. An exercise required in terms of the Open Water training programme is to remain suspended in mid-water, completely motionless while maintaining this position through buoyancy control only. Positive buoyancy can be countered by decreasing lung volume while continuing to breathe shallowly, and conversely, negative buoyancy can be countered by increasing lung volume while breathing shallowly.

Breathing from an alternate air source is an important skill that all divers should learn. It is an essential safety measure used in the event of a diver experiencing a sudden termination of his or her air supply while underwater. The procedure is for the supporting diver to pass his or her spare 'octopus' regulator mouthpiece from the functioning system to the diver requiring air. Sharing a single regulator is another form of buddy breathing; while functional and adequate, it is dangerous and the least desirable way to do so. It should, therefore, only be used in an emergency when no other alternate air supply is available. This form of breathing must be carefully controlled by the buddy with the air supply. He or she should hold the regulator in the right hand and extend it to the diver needing air who, using his or her left hand, guides the regulator into the mouth. At all times the diver with air must maintain possession of the second stage, while the diver without air, using his or her right hand, must hold onto the buddy to ensure that the two do not part. Facing each other and locked into this position, the divers must immediately ascend, observing all necessary decompression procedures.

Safety and problem management form an important part of the Open Water diving programme. Basic First Aid and Cardiopulmonary Resuscitation (CPR) training is given, but divers are advised to do additional courses in both of these subjects, as offered by the Red Cross and similar organizations. Emphasis is placed on avoiding two cardinal enemies of safe diving: panic and overexertion.

The training programme highlights the reality that mistakes do happen and although one may feel ashamed of perpetrating an indiscretion, there must be no hesitation in calling for assistance. There is no virtue in irresponsible or even stoic self-sufficiency while in the realm of a capricious King Neptune who long ago decreed that to dive alone is to die alone! You should always keep a watchful eye on your buddy and on those in your dive group so that you can go to them in the event of them getting into difficulties and vice versa. Divers who are breathing fast and shallowly, whose movements are jerky and whose eyes are wide and unseeing are showing evidence of rising panic. If they are not calmed, it is more than likely that a crisis situation will develop. Before this happens your diagnosis and swift action could help to avert an ugly situation.

In the Open Water course the options open to a diver who is having **breathing difficulties** are explained. The first is to ascend to a shallower depth as this should immediately relieve the situation due to the decrease in pressure during ascent. Breathing will become easier and the decrease in pressure will also 'release' additional air in the tank. Once the diver is able to breathe more freely and equilibrium has been restored, it is advisable for him or her to return to the surface following normal ascent procedures.

◄ *A good diver is one who has learnt to relax completely.*

▼ *Learning to buddy breathe is an essential part of training.*

The second option is to buddy breathe or to breathe from an alternate source, such as an octopus rig, if one is available. When buddy breathing, ascent is immediately initiated and should be continued all the way to the surface. The third option, from depths of 13m (40ft) or less, and one that must be resorted to if your diving buddy is not close by and buddy breathing is not possible, is to make an Emergency Swimming Ascent. Here the diver swims directly for the surface while maintaining neutral lung volume, thereby avoiding rupturing the lungs due to air expansion caused by decreasing pressure. This also reduces the risk of an air embolism. Neutral lung volume is achieved by allowing surplus air to escape from the lungs by making a continuous 'ah' sound on ascent.

If the diver is unable to reach the surface unaided, the normal procedure is to use an Emergency Buoyant Ascent which involves jettisoning weights and inflating the BC to assist in the ascent.

THE BASIC RULES OF SAFE DIVING

▲ *Depth and pressure gauges should be checked regularly.*

The basic rules of safe diving can be summarized as follows:

1. Do not dive if you are not feeling 100% fit – both mentally and physically.
2. Familiarize yourself with the dive site and evaluate the diving conditions. Do not dive if you suspect that conditions may be unfavourable.
3. Do not drink alcohol or take dangerous drugs before diving.
4. Follow the instructions of the Divemaster and make sure you are familiar with the agreed parameters of the dive and the dive's objectives. Plan your participation with your buddy and agree on a general course to follow. Set time and depth limits.
5. Consult the dive tables for each dive, allow for a margin of safety and, if you are an Open Water One diver, plan for a no-decompression dive.
6. Inspect your own and your buddy's equipment prior to the dive.
7. Be prepared for emergencies and ensure that local emergency contact information is on hand.
8. Ensure that you have sufficient weights on your belt to enable you to achieve neutral buoyancy.
   (Remember to check your weights on the surface before diving with new Scuba equipment or when diving in water of a different density than normal.)

9. Always dive with a BC as it makes for easier and safe diving. Remember to inflate it for support while on the surface.
10. Determine likely current direction and strength before diving and take this into account in planning your dive. Always start the dive swimming into the current and do not dive if the current is stronger than one knot, unless it is a drift dive in which case you dive with the current.
11. Limit your maximum depth to 20m (60ft) or less.
12. Check your equipment and SPG frequently, ensuring that at the completion of the dive you have an absolute minimum of 30 bars (440psi) in your tank.
13. Make sure that you pace yourself during the dive, thereby ensuring that you avoid overexertion and breathlessness. Should this occur, stop, rest and make sure that you have fully recovered before proceeding again.
14. Breathe slowly, deeply, and continuously.
15. Exhale slowly and continuously on ascent should the regulator fail to operate or be out of your mouth for any reason.
16. Ascend slowly, at a rate of 10m (33ft) per minute, and be sure that you have a clear and unobstructed vision of the surface. Should your vision be obstructed in any way, hold your hand above your head and keep looking up. Listen for and be watchful of boats on the surface and, immediately upon surfacing, look about you to see if a boat is approaching.
17. As soon as you feel cold or tired, stop diving and do not overextend yourself.
18. Should an emergency situation develop, DO NOT PANIC! Force yourself to relax so that you can think clearly and gain control through appropriate action, thereby avoiding wild and dangerous reaction.

REMEMBER: PLAN YOUR DIVE AND DIVE YOUR PLAN!

Trouble while underwater can also develop from **demand valve failure**. Although this is unusual, it does occur and it is important to know what to do in these circumstances; training in demand valve failure thus forms an important part of the Open Water training course. Most modern regulators are designed to be fail-safe: should any problem occur with the mechanism, it will result in a free flow of air rather than a stopping of the air flow. In this event you should remove the demand valve from your mouth and breathe from it through the lips only, allowing excess air to escape around the edge of the mouthpiece. Never seal your mouth around a free-flowing regulator as the continuous flow of air could 'overfill' your lungs and cause a lung expansion injury. Ascent should be initiated immediately.

Occasionally, particularly if maintenance has been slack and the intricate internal mechanisms of the demand valve have become dirty or rusted, they may jam in such a way that the air supply will shut off and the diver will be unable to draw any air from the tank. In this instance, as when the diver has failed to keep a diligent watch on his or her SPG and run out of air, buddy breathing is imperative and an immediate ascent must be initiated.

Another module in Open Water training is evaluating the **diving environment** and assessing the conditions. Diving is a weather-dependent activity so it is important for the diver to be able to discern suitable conditions, since failure to do so could result in tragedy. Knowledge of weather patterns in the diving area as well as current weather forecasts are a prerequisite for safe diving, particularly if diving should take place in an area of climatic instability. Evaluation of the dive site is necessary and part of Open Water training deals with how to evaluate factors such as currents, tidal conditions, wave action, visibility and area hazards. It is also important to select entry and exit points and to determine entry and exit procedures. This should all be done on arrival at the dive site and prior to kitting up. Should there be any hesitancy or feelings of uncertainty the dive should be abandoned, as it is unlikely to be enjoyable and could quite possibly be dangerous. Tension and diving do not go well together.

▶ *A neutrally buoyant diver 'hovers' above the reef.*

Understanding and using dive tables is an important component of the Open Water training programme. Dive tables indicate the limits within which diving should be done in order to avoid the possibility of getting decompression sickness. Divers should dive well within established limits and use caution if any contributing factors (such as fatigue, cold, age, illness and being overweight) are present. To remove the risk of getting decompression sickness divers must ascend slowly to a designated depth, where they must wait for a specified time to allow for sufficient elimination of any excess nitrogen before resurfacing. This is called decompression diving, which lies beyond the scope of Open Water One. However, since no-decompression diving cannot be guaranteed, training in the principles of decompression diving and the use of appropriate tables is given as part of the Open Water course.

At the successful conclusion of the Open Water training course the trainee should have reached a level of diving proficiency that will enable him or her to participate confidently in safe recreational diving.

ADVANCED DIVER TRAINING

Open Water One certification entitles a diver to enjoy underwater diving in a limited and controlled diving environment. Obviously this qualification is limited in its scope and application and therefore anyone wishing to go beyond the fringes of the exciting world that lies underwater must obtain additional qualifications and experience.

The purpose of the Advanced Diver course is to increase the knowledge, skills and experience of the new aspirant diver for practical application in a wider diving environment. It is essentially a practical training course which provides the trainee with techniques for diving at night, in waters with limited visibility, in deeper water and in less favourable conditions. In addition the course provides an introduction to special interest diving, such as underwater search and light salvage.

The Advanced Diver's course is divided into modules, each of which has three parts: (a) self-study academics; (b) advanced diving skills training; and (c) practical application. In order to enrol, an applicant should have at least an Open Water One qualification and a minimum of 10 logged dives.

At the first open water session of the Advanced Diver training programme, a review of the student's proficiency in basic diving skills is undertaken. However, the instructor may first require a pool session in order to ensure that there is a common understanding of skills terminology and techniques, and that skills proficiency is satisfactory.

The academic curriculum of the Advanced Diver training course examines more fully the physics or natural laws of diving, including:

Buoyancy: Archimedes' Principle is revisited and students are required to state the principle of buoyancy and to calculate buoyancy in fresh water and salt water for various masses. Students must be able to ensure that their buoyancy is correct at all times.

Hydrothermics: The contrast between the heat properties of water to those of air and the effect of water temperature on the human body are explained.

Hydro-optics: The passage of light in water is affected by factors not normally encountered in air. These factors include (1) the diffusion or scattering of light; (2) the blockage of light due to the turbidity of water; (3) the variable absorption of the light waves of the colour spectrum resulting in colour change and intensity underwater; (4) refraction, or the bending of light rays underwater, and its effect of magnifying the size of objects seen underwater.

Hydro-acoustics: Sound is transmitted to the human ear through a medium and the more dense the medium the better and faster the sound will be transmitted. Since water is 800 times more dense than air it is obviously a far better conductor of sound. This is of relevance to the diver since the direction from which sound comes is normally detected by the human brain through the time difference between the arrival of sound waves at first one ear and then the other. However, the time difference between the arrival of sound at the first and then the second ear is hardly perceptible underwater and, as a result, it is extremely difficult to determine sound direction.

Air, Atmospheric Pressure and Pressure/Temperature Relationships: These are re-examined, at the end of which the advanced diver must be able to calculate:

- gauge and absolute pressure for any specified depth in salt or fresh water

- the partial pressure of a gas in a mixture of gases for any given absolute pressure

- the pressure/volume/density relationships of confined gases.

ESSENTIAL ADVANCED DIVER EQUIPMENT

This should include the following:
1. Complete set of underwater equipment, including a wet suit, hood, demand valve with octopus rig, BC, SPG, knife, gloves, and bag.
2. Compass, computer, depth gauge and underwater timing device.
3. Underwater torch.
4. Underwater slate and pencil.

◄◄ *Vertical descent is standard practice on most deep unaided dives.*

◄ *Training in wreck diving is offered by most dive schools.*

NAVIGATION

Training in underwater navigation is an important component of the Advanced Diver training course. It is essential for divers to know where they are underwater and yet navigation is very difficult to achieve due to limited visibility, the absence of references and sensory deprivation resulting from disorientation. The purpose of this training module is to equip the diver with techniques that will enable the diver to know his or her position underwater in relation to a starting point: the first method uses natural surroundings for reference and the second involves using a compass. Underwater navigation is important for the following reasons:

- Careful navigation can prevent the need for long surface swims at the end of the dive.

- A common and planned course helps to keep diving buddies together.

- Specific targets can be reached more easily.

- In poor visibility conditions, good navigation skills are essential.

Good underwater navigation enhances safety and prevents continuous surfacing to ascertain position; known as 'bounce' diving, this is conducive to decompression sickness.

NATURAL NAVIGATION

Natural navigation techniques comprise three separate but related components:

1. Dive patterns
2. Distance estimation
3. Using natural references

Dive Patterns

In the Advanced Diver training course reference is made to a number of dive patterns and their relative advantages and disadvantages. The most obvious, and the most boring, is the **out-and-back** dive pattern in which the divers leave from a starting point and go out to a point where they make a 180-degree turn and return along the same line as the outward journey. In order to add interest to this dive pattern, divers should be able to deviate from it. However, in so doing, deviations should be made at right angles to the agreed dive direction so that getting back to the agreed plan is easier than if deviations are randomly made. Out-and-back dive patterns are used mainly for dives where there is a specific destination such as a wreck or an offshore reef.

◀ *Understanding hydro-optics is particularly important for good photography.*

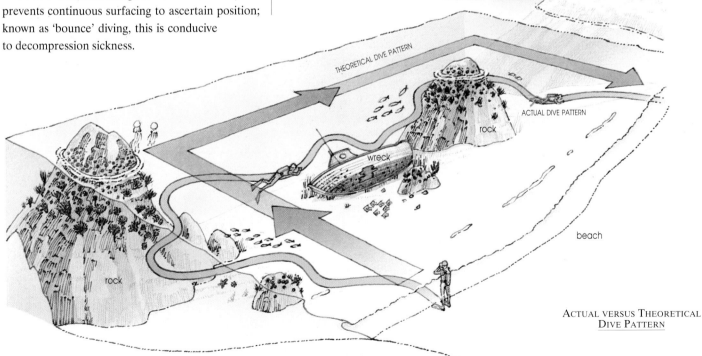

ACTUAL VERSUS THEORETICAL
DIVE PATTERN

Square and **rectangular** dive patterns are more popular since both constantly cover new territory, use desirable right-angle turns and end where they began. **Triangular** dive patterns are not that suitable since they involve greater-than-90-degree turns and these are not that easy to judge, particularly in low-visibility diving conditions. For this reason, this dive pattern is only recommended when a compass is also used.

Circular dive patterns are the most difficult to achieve successfully. It is almost impossible to swim accurately in an arc underwater, unless a compass is used, since it is extremely difficult to know where you are in relation to any other point on the circle.

Distance Estimation
The ability to estimate distances underwater is a very important facility for good and safe diving; it is also useful for relocation of underwater sites and for searching techniques. There are a number of ways in which distance can be estimated – these range from rough approximations to precise measurement. Some of the methods include the following:

Tank pressure The usable air in the tank is divided by the number of segments in the dive pattern, and headings are changed at the respective tank-pressure readings.

This is a fairly accurate way of estimating distance since it takes into account stoppages en route. However, since it really amounts to an apportionment of air to segments of the dive pattern, it does not measure actual distance.

Time is also used to estimate distance. Divers are shown how to calculate their average distance covered per unit of time and this measurement then allows the diver to calculate distances underwater based on the ratio of time to speed. The disadvantage of this method is that it is difficult to take account of stoppages and periods when one slows down to look at something.

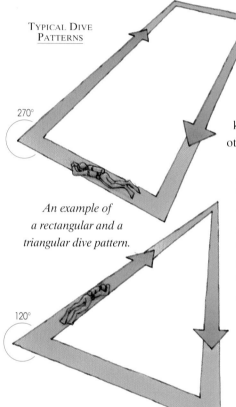

TYPICAL DIVE PATTERNS

270°

120°

An example of a rectangular and a triangular dive pattern.

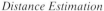

▶ *Kick cycles are just one way of measuring distance underwater.*

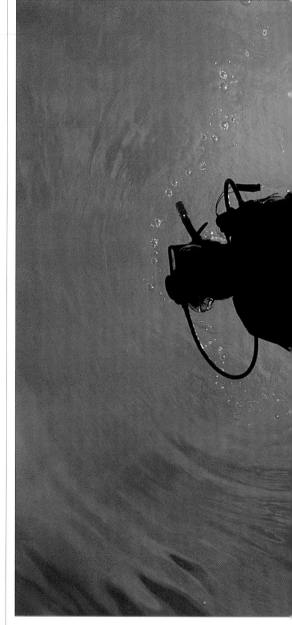

Kick cycles are another way in which to measure distance. A kick cycle is both the upward and downward motion of one leg. The diver must calculate the distance he or she travels through one cycle, and thus by counting the number of cycles, a fairly accurate estimation of distance travelled can be made.

The advantage of this method is that it is possible for the diver to stop and start without dramatically affecting distance calculations. However, the disadvantage is that current strengths and tidal surge can substantially affect the distance travelled per

1. Together with the Divemaster and the other divers, discuss the most suitable dive pattern for the dive site and the dive's objectives. All divers should be in agreement.

2. Divers are taught how to visualize the dive pattern and how to measure one's progress along it. The ability to visualize ahead of time what direction the diver needs to turn in order to remain on a predetermined pattern constitutes an important part of the navigational training module.

3. Emphasis is placed on keeping dive patterns small until divers are comfortable with them and only then expanding the dive area. Confining diving to a relatively small area lessens the risk of members of the diving party becoming lost, becoming overexerted and missing an interesting detail of the dive area.

4. The Advanced Diver course recognizes that deviation from a set plan is inevitable as divers are not expected to dive in a navigational strait-jacket. Divers are thus taught to take note of where they are before deviating and how to get back on course when ready to move on.

5. One diver should be responsible for navigation in a buddy pair, but any change in direction should be agreed to by both partners.

6. Divers are advised that until they are familiar with using dive patterns they should surface when reaching the last stage in order to ascertain whether they are on course or not. This could save a lot of unnecessary swimming should a navigational error have to be corrected.

cycle. It is vitally important, therefore, for the diver to be able to estimate the effect of currents and to make any necessary adjustments.

Arm spans are measured by reaching ahead with one hand and behind with the other, then pivoting on the forward hand and stretching forward again with the freed hand. This is a fairly accurate way of measuring relatively short distances. However, it is difficult to use this method over boulder-strewn, rough or undulating terrain.

Using Natural References
Using natural references in conjunction with dive patterns and reasonably accurate estimations of distances travelled completes the trilogy of natural navigational systems available to the underwater diver. It is important for divers to have some idea of the dive area prior to diving. If it is a familiar site then this is easy, but if not, then every attempt must be made to get as much information as possible from other divers. Failing that, it is important to dive with caution and to observe the natural features

DIVING COMPASS FEATURES

• Diving compasses should be liquid-filled so that they can withstand pressure. The liquid also helps to dampen the movement of the needle, thus reducing rapid swinging back and forth.

• The needle must be able to give an accurate reading even when it is tilted from a level position.

• The compass must have a reference line (the 'lubber' line), extending from side to side across its centre. This line is used for taking bearings and for following headings.

• A useful feature is a bezel which provides rotatable index marks or brackets that can be aligned over the compass needle, thereby providing a fixed heading reference.

• Ideally compasses should have a low profile as they are easier to use.

• A luminous dial is desirable for easy reading in low-light conditions.

▶ *Divers doing a 3m (10ft) decompression stop.*

making up the dive area. Dive references include natural walls, coves, offshore rock formations, kelp beds, coral reefs, wave breaks and tidal surges (which normally run at right angles to the shoreline and therefore are a reliable reference), currents, sand ripples (also a useful reference as they normally run parallel to the shoreline), the angle of the sun (based on the direction that light rays enter the water), and so on. Various plants and animals provide reference information, for example, sea fans, which grow at right angles to the prevailing current and various algae which grow at specific depths. The more aware you are of your underwater surroundings the better you will be able to navigate and the more enjoyable the dive will become.

Also within the navigation training module are the techniques used to locate dive sites. With shore diving, locating the dive site is not really that much of a problem since the position of the dive site bears direct relation to known entry and exit points on the land. However, with offshore diving the use of 'fixes' on the shore is necessary in order to locate the dive site's position. This involves aligning fixed objects on the shore along one heading to the location, and then aligning another set of fixed objects to the location so that the point where the two lines intersect gives the position of the dive site. Tall, thin and clearly discernible landmarks situated at a reasonable distance from one another are the best markers and give the best 'fixes'. The angle between the alignment headings should also be as wide as possible because this improves accuracy in relocation.

COMPASS NAVIGATION
A diving compass is the only reliable navigational tool in water with limited visibility where the bottom is featureless, or in open mid-water where there are no reference points.

During the Advanced Diver training programme, trainees are instructed in how to use a compass, and navigational practice using one is first given on land and then in the open water.

Divers are trained on how to set a diving compass, follow different headings accurately and navigate various dive patterns. Trainees are then required to complete the following tests:

1. To arrive within 8m (25ft) of an object 90m (100yd) distant on which a bearing had been taken.

2. To navigate a square dive pattern with one-minute sides using a compass and to arrive within 8m (25ft) of the starting point.

3. To navigate a triangular dive pattern with one-minute sides using a compass and to arrive within 8m (25ft) of the starting point.

GPS (Global Positioning System) satellite navigation is being adapted for use underwater. While still very expensive, it will no doubt become less so as technology improves and the market develops. This will make underwater navigation very accurate.

LIMITED VISIBILITY AND NIGHT DIVING

The Advanced Diver training course provides the diver with the techniques required for limited visibility and night diving. In both instances a torch or some form of underwater light is necessary, navigation and orientation are important and care must be exercised to ensure constant contact with your buddy. Although limited visibility diving can be unappealing if one is looking for underwater panorama, it need not be so if one is prepared to change one's perspective and focus attention on smaller creatures and specific items of interest. It is often possible to get closer to different forms of aquatic life in lower visibility water, therby enabling the diver to see fascinating creatures and items of interest that might have hidden themselves away in water with better visibility.

An ideal activity in these conditions is close-up photography which nearly always produces spectacular results. Diving techniques, however, are somewhat different in that they embrace slow and deliberate movements with divers 'feeling' their way about, keeping in close touch with tbuddies and, where necessary, using buddy lines to ensure that contact is maintained.

Diving at night is a truly thrilling and exhilarating experience. The majority of aquatic species are nocturnal and places that may seem to be dead by day come alive at night. Many fish that are nervous during the day and dart off in a hurry if you come near often become mesmerized by the diver's light, making it possible to approach them closely. A wide

variety of fish and other marine organisms also come out at night from their hiding places to hunt for food and these add considerably to the range of interest offered by the underwater world. To add to this kaleidoscope of colour and interest, **bioluminescence**, a bluish light given off when diver movement through the water disturbs certain varieties of minute planktonic organisms, creates trails and clusters of little sparkling lights that crisscross and cloud the diving area. In the light of the diver's torch the rich colours of glorious corals, algae and marine organisms stand out in striking contrast to the black waters of the unlit surrounding sea.

▲ *Limited visibility diving often means that fish can be approached closely.*

◀ *Corals stand out brightly against the inky blackness of a night dive.*

SEARCH AND RECOVERY

Search and recovery is a specialized form of diving and therefore lies beyond the scope of the Advanced Diver training course. As a diving speciality, search and recovery involves missions to recover bodies, weapons, forensic evidence, motor vehicles that have crashed off bridges or quaysides, and so on. It should be left to professional teams whose members have been specially trained and who have the necessary equipment to do this type of diving. Having said this, some knowledge and skill in search and recovery is a requirement for every diver since it may be necessary to find and recover diving equipment that has fallen off the dive boat, or a valuable object which may have become lost while diving. Knowing how to search systematically and how to lift reasonably light objects from the sea's floor are valuable skills for any diver to possess. The essential steps required to organize a search and recovery dive are thus taught

in the Advanced Diver programme and include the following: the importance of dive planning, navigation, communications, buoyancy control, and buddy system techniques used in search and recovery. Training in various search patterns appropriate to this level of diving is given, various ways of moving underwater without stirring up silt are explained and practised, and divers are trained in rope tying and how to use a lift bag underwater.

◀ *Using air bags to lift items from the sea bed is part of Advanced Diver training.*

◀◀ *Because of the risks involved, deep diving is only for experienced divers.*

DEEP DIVING

In the Advanced Diver programme, training is given in diving to depths below 18m (60ft), the maximum limit for Open Water One divers. The training programme begins by orientating trainees towards the concept and purpose of deep diving, as the definition of depth is relative to the amount of training and experience the diver has had. For a novice a dive to 20m (66ft) is a deep dive, for an experienced diver it is not. Divers should have a clear purpose or objective for deep diving as this will help to focus attention on predive planning and preparation. Diving without a specific purpose should be limited to depths of 18m (60ft) or less.

The Advanced Diver training programme emphasizes the importance of both psychological and physiological fitness. Panic, anxiety and apprehension are among the greatest risks to safe diving. In the Advanced Diver course, training is given in identifying and coping with the panic syndrome. It is through training and experience that the diver is best equipped to ensure psychological fitness.

REQUIREMENTS FOR DIVEMASTER

The candidate must:

1. Be over 18 years of age.

2. Be an experienced diver with at least one year's intensive diving and an up-to-date log book.

3. Be the holder of an approved Rescue Course.

4. Be fully qualified in cardio-pulmonary resuscitation (CPR).

5. Have an approved First Aid qualification and be 'in date'.

6. Be a competent boat skipper (coxswain) and fully conversant with all forms of boat-shore and inter-boat communication.

7. Be fully conversant with the different types of decompression tables.

8. Know how to use and understand the workings of dive computers.

9. Know all local emergency contacts and how to access emergency services; know where the nearest decompression chamber is and how to get a diver suffering from decompression sickness there in the shortest possible time. Note that the Divemaster is not responsible for divers' decompression profiles; his or her responsibility is to tell the group the depth at which the dive is to be conducted and the likely conditions that will be encountered and it is up to each diver to take responsibility for his or her own dive profiles.

10. Be fully conversant with the workings of all pieces of diving equipment and know how to act in the event of equipment failure.

11. The Divemaster must pass both written and practical examinations in order to lead a diving group.

▶ *Diving in confined spaces requires considerable self-control and experience.*

Although diving is essentially a calm and relaxing sport, physical fitness is an absolute prerequisite since there are moments of high energy output.

In the deep-diving module, the factors influencing the diver's rate of air consumption at depth are explained and the subject of nitrogen narcosis is dealt with in detail. Decompression sickness is also examined. (See Chapter Five for further details.)

The need for additional deep-diving – sometimes referred to as technical diving – equipment is considered in the training course. Increased thermal protection is necessary because of the decrease in water temperature with depth, combined with the additional heat loss due to the higher density of the internally warmed air exhaled by the diver. Thermal considerations are very important in deep diving because of the diver's greater susceptibility, with lowered body temperatures, to decompression sickness. Increased depth will also cause buoyancy loss due to wet-suit compression; therefore, consideration needs to be given to reducing the number of weights the diver carries. The amount will depend on the maximum depth to be attained and the type of exposure suit the diver is wearing. There are two major problems in reducing the weight carried by the diver: firstly, reduced weight makes the initial descent difficult and, secondly, it makes it difficult to maintain a fixed depth if decompression is necessary

during ascent. These problems can be overcome by diving along an anchor line and having extra weights clipped to the line at 3m (10ft), which can then be placed in the pockets of the diver's BC. Depending on the nature of the dive, consideration should also be given to strapping additional tanks with attached demand valves to the line, so that these can be used in the event of an emergency.

Deep diving requires a well-maintained and balanced regulator which will compensate for the increased pressure and greater air density at deeper depths. Having an octopus rig or some other form of alternate air supply is a necessity. Gauges indicating time, depth, direction and air supply are mandatory.

Having completed the Advanced Open Water Diver training course, the trainee is considered to be a trained diver. However, there are higher levels in the training hierarchy – that of Divemaster, followed by Assistant Diving Instructor, Diving Instructor and Master Instructor.

Alternatively, some divers may wish to use their diving skills to pursue a speciality interest such as rescue, search and survey, marine ecology, marine biology, maritime archaeology, cave diving, underwater photography, oceanography, underwater navigation, salvage and recovery and so on (see Chapter Nine). All of the major international diving associations offer training courses in each or most of these areas of speciality interest through their affiliate associations and dive centres.

DIVEMASTER TRAINING

The Divemaster, or Diving Supervisor, is the leader of the dive and is responsible for its planning and all safety aspects. The Divemaster rating is thus the second highest leadership rating and in terms of hierarchy is superseded only by that of Instructor (and Master Instructor). The Divemaster is responsible for the following on each dive:

1. Ensuring that every member of the dive group knows the dive plan.

2. Being in complete control – there is no democracy in diving!

3. Working out the dive profile and impressing upon the diving group the need for them to keep to it. (Should any member of the group disagree with the

◀ *Special training and high qualifications are needed for technical diving.*

dive profile, the Divemaster has the right to ask that person to withdraw from the group. Should there be disagreement and no withdrawal, the Divemaster must publicly refuse to accept responsibility for that person so that the Divemaster cannot be called to task if something goes wrong. It is important to note that each diver is responsible for his or her own dive profile and, unless there is a specific contractual arrangement to the contrary, the Divemaster cannot be held responsible for any mishap.)

4. Checking to ensure that all members' equipment is fully serviceable and that each member has a fully charged diving cylinder.

5. Conducting a detailed predive brief.

6. Carrying the surface marker buoy (SMB).

7. Ensuring that the surface boat is in the hands of a fully competent skipper.

8. Having an 'octopus' rig and ensuring that the dive is so planned that at all times there is sufficient air to carry out an emergency ascent for him- or herself plus an incapacitated diver.

9. Leading the dive and keeping it ordered so that the group remains intact.

10. Ensuring that all divers who enter the water also leave the water, so that no one is lost or left behind.

11. Conducting a debriefing after the dive so that obvious mistakes can be rectified in future, and ensuring that there is an adequate sharing of knowledge and experiences.

DIVING INSTRUCTOR TRAINING

As the name suggests, the Diving Instructor is qualified to teach the sport of diving.

Diving Instructors have to assume a great deal of responsibility. It is their task to take people who are often totally untutored in all aspects of diving and the marine environment and to turn them into competent and confident divers.

The instructor is responsible for the lives of his or her students not only while they are physically on the course, but also in terms of their ability to be safe divers later on. A diving instructor must thus have the discipline to be able to terminate a student's contract if, in his or her opinion, that student will not make a suitable diver.

REQUIREMENTS FOR DIVING INSTRUCTOR

The candidate must:
1. Be over 18 years of age.
2. Hold a Divemaster or Assistant Instructor qualification.
3. Be physically fit.
4. Hold a current CPR and First Aid qualification.
5. Have passed a certified Instructor Training course.
6. Have a minimum of 50 hours of intensive diving in varied conditions, especially in the location in which he or she will be teaching.
7. Be qualified in Rescue and Oxygen Administration and have oxygen available at training sessions.
8. Have access to sufficient fully serviceable equipment for all members of the diving class.
9. Take part in continuing education programmes in order to keep up to date in knowledge and the development of new diving techniques.

CHAPTER FIVE

HEALTH AND SAFETY

It is vital that divers understand how the respiratory and circulatory systems function and how they are affected by diving. It is also important to know the effect pressure has on the air spaces within the human body. However, this chapter is intended only to highlight the scope of information a diver needs to know; further study and practice in basic first aid is necessary for safe diving.

THE RESPIRATORY PROCESS

Respiration involves two basic processes. The first is to draw in oxygen (O_2) from the atmosphere and to deliver it to the cells of the body for metabolic purposes. The second component is to remove carbon dioxide from the body. This takes place through the act of breathing, which has two aspects: external respiration and internal respiration. External respiration refers broadly to the physical act of getting oxygen to the blood and internal respiration to the absorption of O_2 and discharge of CO_2 from the body's cells.

Breathing underwater requires more effort than breathing on land for the following reasons:

- the inhaled air is denser due to increasing pressure
- the external (water) pressure on the chest results in greater resistance to expansion
- the lungs are slightly 'stiffer' due to an increased central blood volume and pooling of blood in the lungs; this reduces the amount of air present
- the resistance to breathing through demand valves.

RESPIRATORY ANATOMY

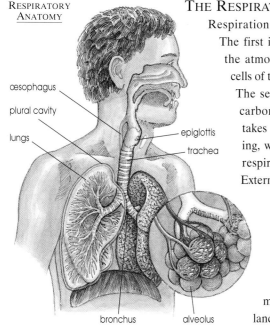

oesophagus

plural cavity

lungs

epiglottis

trachea

bronchus   alveolus

During a surface rescue, it is important to release the patient's weight belt and to inflate the BC to ensure flotation.

All of these factors increase the breathing workload on the diver and emphasize the importance of being physically fit. Divers with heart or lung problems are, therefore, at greater risk of illness or injury. In extreme cases, the air and oxygen supply to the diver may be cut off and the diver may asphyxiate. This may occur due to:

- **drowning** (water blocking the airway)
- **laryngospasm** (the vocal chords closing as a result of irritation by sea water)
- a **foreign body** obstructing the airway
- the diver's **air supply being cut off**
- **breathing carbon monoxide** which prevents oxygen being transported to the tissues.

METABOLISM

Metabolism can essentially be described by the equation:

$$oxygen\ (O_2) + food$$
$$=$$
$$energy + water\ (H_2O) + carbon\ dioxide\ (CO_2)$$

MECHANICS OF BREATHING

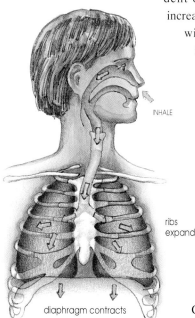

INHALE

ribs
expand

diaphragm contracts

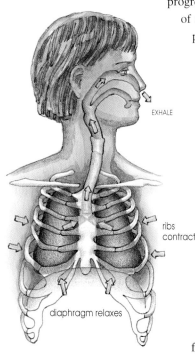

EXHALE

ribs
contract

diaphragm relaxes

▶ *Breath-holding underwater*
is dangerous as it can lead to
carbon dioxide poisoning.

BREATHING RESISTANCE

Air flow through the airways of the lung is dependent on the density of the breathed gas. With increasing depth the density of air increases along with the resistance to air flow causing an increased workload on the diver. Most healthy divers have considerable reserves in breathing capacity and this increase is seldom noticed until 30m (100ft) in depth or a pressure of 4atm(a).

Divers should remember that any added resistance to air flow through diving regulators or demand valves adds to the above naturally occurring resistance and further increases the workload. They should thus ensure that their demand valve is functioning normally and is appropriate for diving at the planned depth.

CARBON DIOXIDE TOXICITY

Carbon dioxide builds up in the body (**hypercapnia**) as a result of physical exertion and inadequate ventilation of the lungs. As this happens a progression of effects takes place. Initially, the rate of respiration increases and respiration becomes progressively more difficult until, at a very high concentration of carbon dioxide, dizziness sets in, followed by stupor and unconsciousness. Inadequate ventilation (**hypoventilation**) results from unconscious changes in the breathing pattern usually caused by anxiety or apprehension.

It is important to note that the ability to discharge carbon dioxide from the respiratory system varies from person to person. Shallow rapid breathing, particularly during exertion, must be avoided and an adequate air flow from the diver's air cylinder must be maintained. It is also important to avoid **skip breathing**, a practice often used by scuba divers to extend their bottom time, and by underwater photographers, where the divers hold their breath for a number of seconds to reduce movement. This is extremely dangerous as carbon dioxide build-up increases with breath-holding and its adverse effects may result in a sudden loss of consciousness. Divers who experience throbbing headaches after diving are probably skip breathing.

OVEREXERTION

The effects of overexertion are not immediately felt as there is a delay between actual exertion and the additional oxygen required to meet its demands. On land, the adjustment required to meet this delay represents no problem, but underwater the extra heavy breathing required to supply the necessary oxygen cannot be met within the constraints of normal regulators. The result is a sensation of suffocation and immediate anxiety which can easily give way to panic if the diver is not very careful. Obviously prevention is the best solution and therefore divers should, at all times, try to avoid situations where overexertion could result. Should this not be possible, at the first indication of laboured breathing the diver must stop all activity and rest by hanging on to a rock, or by deeply wedging the blades of his or her fins into sand and allowing breathing to return to normal. Only return to the surface if breathing difficulties persist; it should then be done slowly and strictly in accordance with normal ascent procedures. Often at a shallower depth, equilibrium is re-established and the diver may proceed with the dive, provided precautions are taken against further overexertion.

Factors that contribute to overexertion include wasted effort, a malfunctioning regulator and excessive cold. If you are out of breath underwater you are, without a doubt, doing something wrong!

HYPERVENTILATION AND SHALLOW-WATER BLACKOUT

Hyperventilation results from excessively rapid and deep breathing which lowers the carbon dioxide level in the body below normal, thereby producing a condition known as **hypocapnia**. This normally results in a feeling of lightheadedness and if hyperventilation continues it will extend to general weakness, a feeling of being faint and a blurring of vision. Since it is the build-up of carbon dioxide in the lungs that triggers the message to the brain to breathe, an artificial lowering of that level will result in a delay in the perceived need to breathe. The diver's blood oxygen may, therefore, drop below the level necessary to keep him or her conscious before the carbon dioxide level rises to a point which stimulates the diver to want to breathe. The diver blacks out and becomes unconscious. This is known as **shallow-water blackout** or **hypoxia of ascent**.

Extended breath-holding following hyperventilation normally results from anxiety or physical stress and could result in unconsciousness or muscle spasms. If you notice that you are breathing excessively fast, forcibly slow your breathing rate down and make yourself relax.

CARBON MONOXIDE POISONING

Carbon monoxide (CO) readily combines with blood haemoglobin to form carboxyhaemoglobin, which restricts the haemoglobin's capacity to transport sufficient oxygen to the body tissues. This condition in turn results in hypoxia (oxygen starvation). In order to avoid carbon monoxide poisoning it is absolutely essential to ensure that the air inlet to compressors used to fill diving cylinders is well away from any source of contamination.

OXYGEN TOXICITY

Oxygen, if breathed at a partial pressure of greater than 1.4atm, can be poisonous to the lung and brain tissues. Lung toxicity is a more chronic event and is not normally seen in sports divers. Brain toxicity, however, is common and manifests when breathing

---

GENERAL PRINCIPLES OF FIRST AID

THE BASIC PRINCIPLES OF FIRST AID INCLUDE:

• doing no harm
• sustaining life
• preventing deterioration
• promoting recovery

In the event of any illness or injury, a simple sequence of patient assessment and management can be followed. The first things to check are commonly known as the ABCs:

A: AIRWAY
B: BREATHING
C: CIRCULATION
D: DECREASED level of consciousness
E: EXPOSURE

Ensure both the patient's and your own safety by removing yourselves from the threatening environment (usually the water). Do not further endanger the patient or yourself.

NEVER ASSUME THAT THE PATIENT IS DEAD.

Check the ABCs as follows:

A: AIRWAY
1. Is there a neck injury?
2. Are the mouth and nose free of obstruction? Noisy breathing is a sign of airway obstruction.

B: BREATHING
1. Look to see if the chest is rising and falling.
2. Listen for air moving at the nose and mouth.
3. Feel for air moving against your cheek.

C: CIRCULATION
1. Feel for a pulse next to the windpipe.

D: DECREASED LEVEL OF CONSCIOUSNESS
1. Does the patient respond to any of the following procedures (AVPU):

   A) Is the patient **awake**, aware, spontaneously speaking?
   V) Does the patient respond to **verbal stimuli**, ie: a loud call to 'Wake up!'?
   P) Does the patient respond to **painful stimuli**, ie: to a sharp pinch or slap?
   U) Is the patient totally **unresponsive**?

E: EXPOSURE
In order to examine the patient properly remove clothes as necessary.

NOW SEND FOR HELP.

If you think the patient's condition is serious, send or call for help from the emergency medical services (ambulance, paramedics). Whoever you send to get help should return to confirm that help is indeed on its way.

---

pure (100%) oxygen at depths greater than 6m (20ft) of sea water (msw) or air deeper than 67m (220ft). The advent of Nitrox diving (increased oxygen percentage in the breathing mixture) will, if not used correctly, inevitably increase the incidence of brain oxygen toxicity. The clinical presentation of oxygen toxicity is often sudden and unpredictable resulting in unconsciousness and seizures which can be catastrophic underwater. In the case of oxygen toxicity, prevention is definitely better than cure.

RECOVERY POSITION

If the patient is unconscious but breathing normally, there is a risk of vomiting and subsequent choking. It is therefore critical that the patient be turned onto the side in the recovery position.

1. Place the patient's left hand under the head with the palm forwards (facing up).

2. Cross the patient's right leg over the left ankle.

3. Fold the right arm over the chest.

4. Grasp the right hip and pull the patient over onto the side with your left hand, supporting the patient's left cheek with the right hand.

5. Flex the patient's right knee to 90˚.

6. Flex the patient's right arm to 90˚ and place the forearm flat on the ground.

7. The patient is now in a stable recovery position.

If the patient is unconscious and cannot protect his or her airway, he or she must be turned carefully onto the side despite possible spinal injury. Be sure to immobilize the patient in a straight line first.

HYPERTHERMIA

A rise in body temperature results from a combination of overheating (due to exercise, exposure to heat or overinsulation) and inadequate fluid intake. The diver will progress through heat exhaustion to heat stroke with eventual collapse. Heat stroke is a serious illness and if the diver is not cooled and rehydrated immediately, he or she can die.

The diver should be removed from the hot environment and all clothes taken off. Sponge the patient with a damp cloth and fan either manually or with an electric fan. If the patient is conscious, he or she can be given fluids orally. If unconscious, place the patient in the recovery position and monitor the ABCs. Always seek medical help thereafter.

HYPOTHERMIA

Normal internal body temperature is just under 37˚C (98.6˚F). If for any reason it is pushed much below this – usually through inadequate protective clothing – progressively more serious symptoms may occur, with death as the ultimate result.

• A 1˚C (2˚F) drop causes shivering and discomfort.

• A 2˚C (3˚F) drop induces the body's self-heating mechanisms to react; blood flow to the peripheries is reduced and shivering becomes extreme.

• A 3˚C (5˚F) drop leads to amnesia, confusion, disorientation, heartbeat and breathing irregularities, and possibly rigor.

The patient should be moved to a sheltered, warm area or further heat loss should be prevented by wrapping him or her in a space blanket, surrounding the diver with you and your buddies' bodies, and covering his or her head and neck with a woolly hat, warm towels or anything suitable. In sheltered warmth, re-dress the diver in warm, dry clothing and then put him or her in a space blanket.

If the diver is conscious and coherent, a warm shower or bath and a warm, sweet drink should be adequate treatment. If it isn't, call the emergency services and treat for shock while deploying the other warming measures mentioned. It is important to note that the application of sudden heat to the patient (eg: a hot water bottle) could cause him or her to go into shock.

NEAR DROWNING

Near drowning is the term used to describe the clinical condition that follows the aspiration of fluid into the lungs, while **drowning** occurs when this results in death. Indications of near drowning include **cyanosis** (skin turns blue), the cessation of breathing and frothing at the mouth. The aspiration of fluid into the lungs results in oxygen starvation (hypoxia) which may cause permanent brain tissue damage after four to five minutes, although this may be lengthened in extremely cold conditions.

Self-control is required when choking: the cutoff of air can lead to panic and the inhalation of more water, creating a vicious circle. Contain your coughing as much as possible. Do not remove the regulator from your mouth, instead cough into it. Swallowing several times can also help.

Near drowning can occur when water enters the larynx and causes a spasm of the vocal chords that blocks the airway, resulting in asphyxiation; this is generally known as 'dry' near drowning. If water fills the lungs, this is known as 'wet' near drowning.

When near drowning does occur, various physiological changes may take place, depending on whether it happens in fresh water or sea water. In the case of fresh water, the blood is diluted as a result of osmosis through the alveolar membranes since fresh water is **hypotonic** (less salty than blood).

Dilution leads to disintegration of blood cells and changes in the blood's chemistry. If the lungs are filled with sea water, which is **hypertonic** (saltier than blood), the blood thickens as fluids leave the blood by osmosis, thus diluting the fluid in the lungs. In either case hypoxia and injury to the lungs result. Water in the lungs may lead to **secondary drowning** due to changes in blood volume and blood chemistry brought about by osmosis. If the victim is unconscious and not breathing, artificial respiration must be applied immediately. The patient's pulse must be checked and CPR administered if necessary. Cognizance must be taken of the fact that the detection of a pulse on a cold and unconscious diver can be difficult. Administer oxygen via a non-rebreather mask as soon as possible if available. Continue oxygen administration even when the patient begins to breathe independently. A diver who has inhaled a significant volume of water should be taken to hospital immediately and kept there under observation, even if he or she is feeling fine and is apparently breathing freely.

▼ *Buddy support is essential during an emergency.*

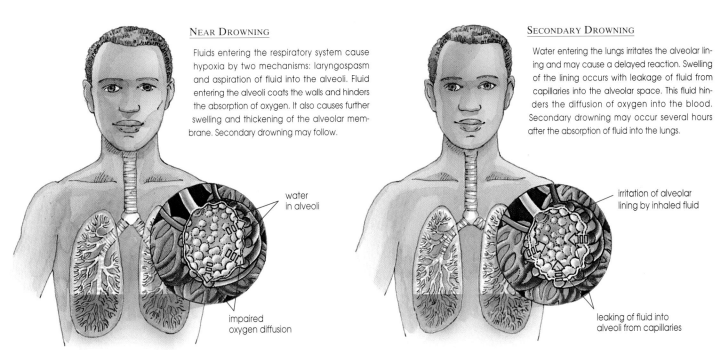

NEAR DROWNING

Fluids entering the respiratory system cause hypoxia by two mechanisms: laryngospasm and aspiration of fluid into the alveoli. Fluid entering the alveoli coats the walls and hinders the absorption of oxygen. It also causes further swelling and thickening of the alveolar membrane. Secondary drowning may follow.

water in alveoli

impaired oxygen diffusion

SECONDARY DROWNING

Water entering the lungs irritates the alveolar lining and may cause a delayed reaction. Swelling of the lining occurs with leakage of fluid from capillaries into the alveolar space. This fluid hinders the diffusion of oxygen into the blood. Secondary drowning may occur several hours after the absorption of fluid into the lungs.

irritation of alveolar lining by inhaled fluid

leaking of fluid into alveoli from capillaries

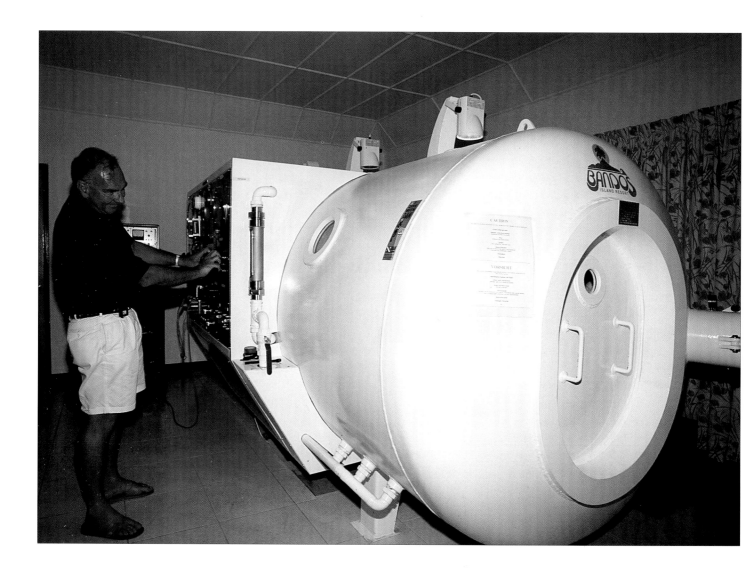

▲ Divers should always know where the nearest recompression chamber is located.

NITROGEN NARCOSIS

Under normal conditions nitrogen is an inert gas, but when breathed under pressure it induces narcosis or anaesthesia due to some (not fully understood) interactions of the gas with nerve cells. Narcosis, or 'raptures of the deep' as it is poetically known, tends to become more evident at depths approaching 30m (100ft), which is why recreational diving is limited to a maximum of 40m (130ft). The initial symptoms are not that dissimilar to those resulting from hypoxia, and become more severe with depth. They range from an impairment of reasoning, thought and judgment to an inability to perform mental or motor skills. Another symptom associated with narcosis which affects some divers is a feeling of elation and well-being, while others feel apprehension and anxiety. Some divers may present no symptoms at all.

Although the symptoms are inconsistent and may seem to be fairly harmless, narcosis is a significant diving hazard because it increases the risk of an accident while reducing the diver's ability to cope with an emergency. It may also hide the signs or symptoms of hypocapnia and overexertion and it may cause the diver to read his or her gauges incorrectly, resulting in incorrect decompression decisions. Narcosis comes on quickly, but fortunately also goes equally quickly on ascending to a shallower depth (normally above 30m; 100ft – or 4 bar[a]).

A diver's susceptibility to nitrogen narcosis increases with anxiety, exertion, being physically fatigued, while diving with a hangover, while under medication, or in poor visibility, cold water and poor environmental conditions.

DECOMPRESSION SICKNESS (DCS OR 'THE BENDS')

Nitrogen dissolves in the body's tissues in equilibrium with its ambient partial pressure. As the diver descends, the ambient pressure increases and more gas enters the tissues than is eliminated. Since the nature of tissue in the human body differs between the brain, heart, bones, muscles, blood and fatty tissues, their gas absorption and elimination rates differ. Absorption consists of a number of stages: first is the transfer of inert gas (nitrogen) from the lungs to the blood, then from the blood to the various tissues through which the blood flows. The force that drives the absorption process (known as the **gradient**) is the partial pressure difference of the gas between the lungs and the blood, and between the blood and body tissue. As the gradient between the blood and body tissue equalizes, the tissue reaches **saturation**. The **rate** of saturation depends on the volume of blood flowing through the tissues and their mass. Bone cartilage, for example, reaches saturation far more slowly than brain tissue. During ascent, elimination of nitrogen takes place in a process known as **outgassing**. The rate of elimination is determined by the rate of blood flow, the difference in the partial pressures and the amount of nitrogen dissolved in the tissues and blood.

For safe diving, a careful balance has to be maintained. This is achieved by combining diving depth, bottom time and the rate of ascent within safe limits. Should this not be done, the required elimination of dissolved nitrogen will not take place; instead, bubbles of nitrogen will form either in the bloodstream – in which case they block circulation – or in body tissue – in which case they distort the tissue as the gas expands with decreased ambient pressure. Symptoms depend on the location of the bubbles:

Epidermal DCS or skin bends: the skin itches or even burns and mottled patches can develop all over the body. An accompanying rash normally disappears after a couple of hours.

Muscularskeletal DCS or joint bends: the most common form of decompression sickness, normally affecting large joints like the shoulder and elbow. It consists of sharp pain that slowly reaches a climax, sometimes hours after the dive, and then subsides spontaneously some hours later.

Central nervous system bends: affects the spinal cord (spinal DCS) or brain (cerebral DCS) and can cause permanent damage. It is important to recognize the early symptoms of a spinal bend which usually begins with back pain that may radiate around the abdomen ('girdle' pain). This is then followed by a feeling of 'pins and needles' in the legs, which become unsteady. Urination is difficult and eventually paralysis below the neck or waist develops.

Brain damage from cerebral DCS is rare but does occur, as does inner ear bends in which the patient becomes dizzy and cannot balance properly.

ANATOMY OF THE EAR

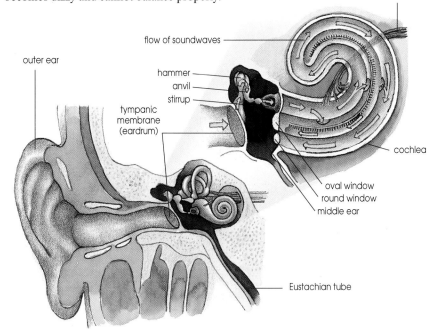

auditory nerve
flow of soundwaves
outer ear
hammer
anvil
stirrup
tympanic membrane (eardrum)
cochlea
oval window
round window
middle ear
Eustachian tube

Chokes: a rare illness characterized by an acute shortness of breath, chest pains and a cough. Unless treated with recompression therapy it is possible that the victim will suffer circulatory collapse and death. The chokes normally evolves after rapid and uncontrolled ascent from a deep dive.

The treatment of divers suffering from DCS consists of recompressing the patient while he or she breathes 100% oxygen. The diver is then slowly decompressed at a rate that will allow for the full elimination of all excess nitrogen without further formation of nitrogen bubbles. This must be carried out in a hyperbaric chamber and should not be attempted through resubmergence.

DCS AND DIVE TABLES

The English physiologist Haldane, working in the late 19th century, was the first person to develop a set of dive tables designed to establish safe limits within which single dives and repetitive dives could be conducted on the same day without the diver incurring decompression sickness.

The Haldane tables have since been modified and new theories and ideas on gas absorption and elimination have been developed. These theories have, in turn, led to modifications of the Haldane tables and to the establishment of new ones, each setting safer standards than those before.

However, no dive table is foolproof or completely safe because each diver is different, and each diver's physical and emotional condition varies from day to day, while diving conditions change from place to place and from hour to hour. Divers should be aware that most of the tables that are available today, especially those based on naval tables such as the US Navy and the Royal Navy, are calculated on a maximum of two dives per day (ie: one repetitive dive) and not multiple dives.

Remember that while dive tables may indicate that you are within the limits set by mathematical formulae, your body may not conform. It is also important to recognize the limitations of computers as a means of controlling decompression diving.

Great care should also be taken on diving holidays in order to prevent excessive **nitrogen build-up**. Ideally you should limit your dives to two per day and start each new day with the deepest dive first. After three days of diving, stop and take a day off. This will allow the nitrogen built up in the tissues to dissipate completely and diving can recommence on the fifth day with no nitrogen build-up in the body. Multi-dive days and multi-day diving are two of the most common causes of DCS in diving resorts.

Care must also be exercised, especially with repetitive diving, to avoid **dehydration**. Nitrogen retention is an insidious enemy that steadily builds up, particularly in those tissues that saturate more slowly and correspondingly eliminate nitrogen more slowly. Research scientists are finding increasing evidence that dehydration has an important influence on decompression sickness, since it causes the blood to slow down (stasis) as a result of thickening, thus resulting in poor blood flow through tissues and poor elimination of nitrogen.

The most common causes of dehydration are **sea sickness**, **alcohol** and **excessive perspiring**. A diver that vomits prior to a dive should rather not dive and a diver vomiting after the dive must drink fluids as soon as possible. Alcohol is a diuretic and a diver who has had a significant amount to drink the previous evening should ensure that he or she drinks plenty of fluids before diving or does not dive. Excessive perspiring can lead to dehydration; therefore strenuous exercise prior to diving must be avoided.

Another factor that should be considered very carefully by divers is **flying** after diving. The most widely accepted guidelines for flying after diving are those set out by DAN (Divers Alert Network):

• For a single daily no-decompression-stop dive, wait 12 hours.

• For multiple no-decompression-stop dives on single or consecutive days, a 12–24-hour wait is the recommended guideline.

• For any dives where compulsory decompression stops were done, a period of greater than 24 hours extending to as much as 48 hours is recommended.

Cabin pressure in a passenger aircraft is set to an altitude of between 1500 and 3000m (4900–9800ft) above sea level, which is quite sufficient to cause DCS if a diver flies too soon.

Each organization has its own set of dive tables.

CARDIOPULMONARY RESUSCITATION (CPR)

Cardiopulmonary resuscitation is required when a patient is found to have no pulse. It consists of techniques to:

VENTILATE THE PATIENT'S LUNGS (expired air resuscitation)

PUMP THE PATIENT'S HEART (external cardiac compression)

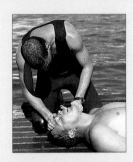

A. Airway

1. Gently extend the head (head tilt) and lift the chin with two fingers (chin lift). This will lift the tongue away from the back of the throat and open the airway.
2. If you suspect a foreign body in the airway, sweep your finger across the back of the tongue from one side to the other. If an obstruction is found, remove it. Do not attempt this on a conscious or semiconscious patient as he or she may either bite your finger or vomit.

B. Breathing

If the patient is not breathing you need to give expired air resuscitation, in other words, you need to breath into the patient's lungs:

1. Pinch the patient's nose closed.
2. Place your mouth, open, fully over the patient's mouth, making a good seal.
3. Exhale into the patient's mouth hard enough to cause the patient's chest to rise.
4. If the patient's chest fails to rise, you need to adjust the position of the airway. The 16% of oxygen in your expired air is adequate to sustain life.
5. Initially, give two full, slow breaths.
6. If the patient is found to have a pulse at this stage, continue breathing for the patient once every five seconds, checking for a pulse after every 10 breaths.
7. If the patient begins breathing independently, place in the recovery position.

C. Circulation

If, after giving two breaths, no pulse is found you need to give external cardiac compression.

1. Kneel next to the patient's chest.
2. Measure two finger breadths above the notch where the ribs meet the lower end of the breast bone.
3. Place the heel of your right hand just above your two fingers in the centre of the breast bone.
4. Place the heel of your left hand on your right hand.
5. Straighten your elbows.
6. Place your shoulders perpendicularly above the patient's breast bone.
7. Compress the breast bone 4–5cm (1.5–2in) to a rhythm of 'one, two, three...'
8. Give 15 compressions.

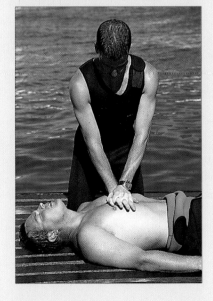

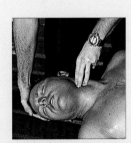

Continue giving cycles of two breaths and 15 compressions, checking for a pulse after every five cycles. The aim of CPR is to keep the patient alive until the paramedics or a doctor arrives with the necessary equipment. Make sure that you and your buddy are trained in CPR – it could be the difference between life and death.

BAROTRAUMA

Within the human body there are a number of air-filled spaces which can be damaged if the pressure within those spaces is not equalized with ambient pressure. This is known as **barotrauma**. Areas involved are the middle ear, the paranasal sinuses, the lungs and airways, and the gastrointestinal tract.

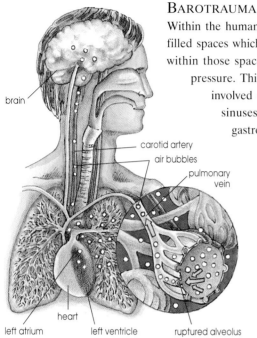

brain

carotid artery

air bubbles

pulmonary vein

heart

left atrium   left ventricle   ruptured alveolus

AIR EMBOLISM

LUNG BAROTRAUMA

The main cause of lung barotrauma is the failure to permit expanding air in the lungs to escape during ascent. By not exhaling during a Scuba diving ascent, the lungs overexpand as the pressure within the lungs is greater than ambient pressure. This causes the lung alveoli to distend and eventually rupture, which may result in the possible entry of alveolar gas into the pulmonary venous system.

The gas is then carried to the heart and from there into the major arteries where it may cause a gas blockage or restriction (**embolus**).

The signs and symptoms of an air embolism, which usually occur immediately after surfacing, are determined by its position. If circulation to the heart is cut off, then the symptoms produced are similar to a heart attack. If it is in the arteries leading to the brain, dizziness, a lack of coordination, convulsions, paralysis, unconsciousness, and even death may be the result.

At the sign of the first symptom, first aid should be administered. The patient should be laid in the recovery position and 100% oxygen administered while arrangements are made to evacuate the diver to the nearest resuscitation facility and recompression chamber. Recompression is the only effective means of treating this illness. Do not attempt to recompress the diver underwater. Artificial respiration or CPR may be necessary.

Some other causes of lung rupture and consequent embolism include asthma and damage done by cigarette smoking.

EAR BAROTRAUMA

When ambient pressure is increased without a corresponding increase in pressure within the middle ear, the tympanic membrane (eardrum) bulges inward and may rupture. In addition, the tissue of the middle ear swells and some minor bleeding may occur causing damage to the sensitive structures in the middle ear. To prevent this trauma, equalize the middle ear immediately the descent commences, using one or a combination of the equalization manoeuvres (Valsalva, Frenzel or Toynbee) taught in the basic scuba course. Do not wait for pain to develop first. Should any discomfort be felt, ascend and clear your ears, then continue descending.

Failure to equalize pressure in the middle ear creates a pressure differential across the tympanic membrane and this can cause it to rupture. However, overforceful equalization of the middle ear could result in damage to the inner ear causing vertigo and ringing in the ears.

If the discomfort continues, you should terminate your dive immediately and seek prompt treatment from an ear, nose and throat specialist who understands diving injuries.

SINUS BAROTRAUMA

Sinus barotrauma is caused by a blockage of the air passages to the paranasal sinuses and results in sinus squeeze with painful swelling and bleeding. Sinus squeeze can be avoided by not diving while suffering from a cold, an allergy attack or any form of nasal congestion. Sinuses are equalized as for the middle ear by the Valsalva Manoeuvre.

DENTAL BAROTRAUMA

Cavities in one's teeth caused by tooth decay or poor fillings can lead to pressure differentials and tooth squeeze. Diving should be terminated if dental discomfort is experienced, and a dentist consulted.

EAR BAROTRAUMA

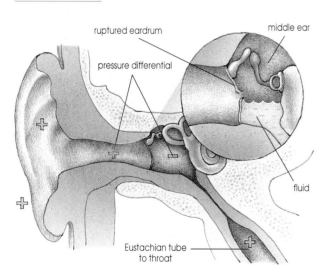

ruptured eardrum

middle ear

pressure differential

fluid

Eustachian tube to throat

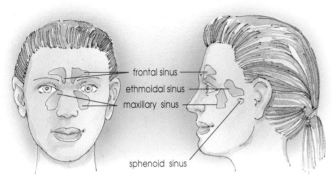

SINUS BAROTRAUMA

GASTROINTESTINAL BAROTRAUMA

Certain foods produce excessive gas during the digestive process and if there is a restriction of the movement of this gas, discomfort will result as it expands during ascent. In severe instances this situation can result in the rupture of the bowel tissue. Divers should refrain from eating gas-producing food and from drinking fizzy drinks before diving, or from swallowing air while diving. Divers experiencing this form of barotrauma should descend in order to relieve any discomfort and then slowly re-ascend.

CRAMPS

Cramp occurs when a muscle goes into spasm as a result of dehydration and blood salt abnormalities. This can be caused by exertion or overuse of a muscle, cold, fatigue, poor nutrition and poor health. Onset normally begins with a twinge of the affected muscle, and relief is effected by temporarily ceasing

DENTAL BAROTRAUMA

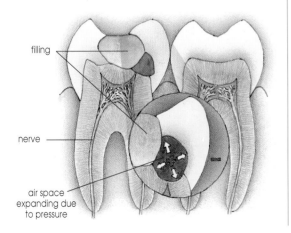

filling

nerve

air space expanding due to pressure

to use the affected muscle, and by stretching and massaging it. Cramp often occurs in the calf muscle. To relieve this, hold the tip of your fin and straighten your leg while pulling upwards on the fin. Once the cramp has gone, rest the muscle for a while and then proceed at a slower pace.

CAROTID SINUS REFLEX

The main arteries carrying blood to the brain are the carotid arteries. These have a small bulge (sinus) at the fork of the artery in the neck which controls the heart rate according to blood pressure. Should a tight hood or the neck seal of a dry suit apply pressure to the carotid sinuses, it could lead to faintness, especially when exertion is involved. This can be avoided by the careful selection of your dry suit and diving hood.

SUDDEN DEATH SYNDROME

Diving requires a certain amount of exertion and sometimes produces a measure of tension. These factors increase the workload of the heart and may result in a heart attack with sudden death. Divers are advised to have a full diving medical by a diving physician before commencing the sport.

▼ *Cramp is relieved by stretching the affected muscle.*

CHAPTER SIX

THE SEA AND ITS MANY MOODS

The sea operates on its own terms; misreading its mood can result in an unpleasant and wasted dive, costly mistakes, or even death. Understanding the sea and familiarizing yourself with local conditions will make for safer and richer diving.

WAVE ACTION

Waves provide the first indication of the sea's mood. If they are dark and lumpy and the swells are short, then diving is unlikely to be good; if the sea is flat or the swells are long and the waves rounded and regular, then the chances are that diving conditions will be fine. Waves move in accordance with the direction of the prevailing wind; they are also influenced by geological action and the gravitational influences of the sun and moon. The **height** of the wave is the vertical distance from its crest to its trough; the **length** of a wave is the horizontal distance between two successive crests (or troughs); and the **period** of the wave is the time it takes for two successive crests to pass a given point.

Many people mistakenly believe that a passing wave transports water forward, but this is not the case as the water actually circulates while the wave of energy passes through. The water particles within a wave move in an orbit equivalent to the wave height, returning to virtually the same position once the wave has passed. These orbits are repeated

WAVE TERMINOLOGY

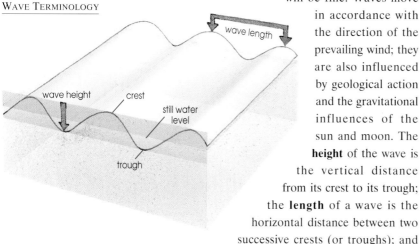

Not all dive sites are suitable at all times and seasons; care should be taken to check prevailing conditions.

underwater but become smaller and smaller as the influence of the wave diminishes. Thus objects are not transported by wave action, but rather by wind action on the surface and by currents underwater. Wind creates waves in two ways: by changing air pressure and by creating frictional drag on the surface. Initially small ripples are created, but these evolve into waves of increasing dimension as the wind's velocity increases over the **fetch** (the area over which the wind blows), and this results in more energy being transferred directly from the air to the water. The waves continue to grow in height in direct relation to the wind velocity until they are so steep that they eventually topple over, forming white

LAUNCHING THROUGH THE SURF

Tidal movement and wave action are important factors to be considered in launching a dive boat from the beach. During high tide, wave action is likely to be too high for safe launching and at low tide, shallow reefs could become a problem. Skill and precise timing is required to pilot a boat through breaking waves.

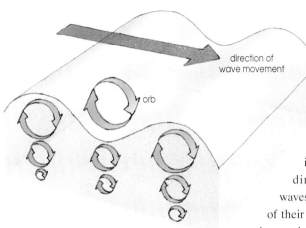

ORBITAL WAVE MOVEMENT

caps. When wind velocity remains constant or dies down, the waves stabilize and a swell will develop.

A **swell** is a wave that is fairly constant in height, period and direction. In this form, waves can retain virtually all of their energy and travel many thousands of kilometres.

Once normal waves move into water that is shallower than one half of a wavelength, the sea's floor begins to pull on the orbital motion of the water within the waves. This causes the orbits to flatten into ellipses and, with the inertia of the wave's energy driving it forward and the drag of the sea floor pulling it backwards, a back-and-forth motion known as **surge** develops.

Surge is strongest when the water is shallow, the waves large and the wave length long. For divers, it is an important factor as it sweeps the diver backwards and forwards producing unpleasant and possibly dangerous conditions.

SURF

As a wave nears the shore and the water becomes shallower, the bottom portion of the wave is slowed up by friction while the top portion continues at its previous speed. When the depth is approximately twice the wave height, the crest of the wave begins to steepen towards a peak and the wave velocity and wave length decreases. At a depth of about 1.3 times the height of the wave its peak begins to incline forward at a greater-than-60° angle; as it curls over and plunges forward the wave becomes unstable. The orbit within the wave collapses, the water moves with the wave and forms an area of white water caused by bubbles of air being captured in the water. This is known as **surf** and is the zone where the waves give up their energy and the wave's ordered motion gives way to broken turbulence. The momentum of the broken water carries it onto the beach where the water's remaining energy is finally dissipated on its rush up the shore. The water transported up the beach is unbalanced, so as soon as its forward motion stops it flows back to the sea as a backwash.

▶ *When entering the sea through surf, it is best to do so backwards.*

As a general rule, **breaking waves** approach in sets of smaller waves followed by a group of larger waves. This variation in wave height and strength is due to wave swells from slightly different directions combining and reinforcing one another, thereby producing waves higher than those of either individual wave swell. Divers doing a shore entry must study the wave pattern in the area so that they time their entry (or exit) to coincide with a period of low wave action. They should also study the surf zone: if it is wide it is because the beach slopes gradually. This means that the strength of the waves has been reduced as waves progressively release their energy.

Entry can be made relatively easily by backing into the water until it becomes possible to snorkel and swim out beyond the wave break. Dive under incoming waves to avoid the wave's orbit of energy.

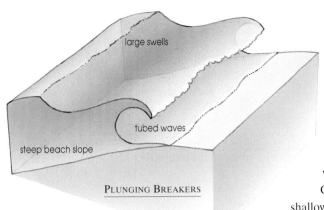

PLUNGING BREAKERS

If the surf zone is narrow, it normally means that the beach slopes steeply which makes a shore entry more hazardous for a fully equipped diver. Here, the surf is formed by large swells over a moderately steep bottom and

as the swell moves towards the shore, the waves steepen, breaking suddenly and with tremendous force. These **plunging breakers** release their energy quickly and can easily knock a standing diver over. Timing of entry is absolutely critical and it is imperative to move away from the surf zone as quickly as possible and into deeper water where the wave's strength is reduced.

Caution must be exercised with entry over shallow rocks or coral reefs as incoming waves can become liquid battering rams, pounding a diver mercilessly against rocks, often encrusted with barnacles, or against rugged corals with their razor-sharp and toxic edges.

Exiting through the surf also requires careful timing. Divers should stop before the surf zone and observe the wave patterns in order to select the biggest wave from a large set and then to ride in on its back. It is important to have your mask on at all times so that you can observe conditions easily. Make sure that you hold it in place as the sea may rip it from your face. Once reaching waist-deep water, on beaches that slope gradually, stand and face the incoming waves. With your knees bent, shuffle towards the shore; duck beneath any wave that is more than chest high.

On steeper beaches it is again important to select a large wave and to ride in on its back, making sure that you neither get sucked into it nor get ahead of it, causing you to end up in the break zone. With careful timing and judicious selection it is possible to have the wave deposit you on the beach. Then, stand up and secure your footing so that you can withstand the strong backwash. After this, clear away from the wash zone as quickly as possible. Never ride a wave up and over rocks as this could be dangerous due to a possible sudden drop of the wave which may pull a diver back into the trough, resulting in him or her being deposited onto the rocks and battered by the next pounding wave.

SPILLING BREAKERS

THE TIDE CYCLE

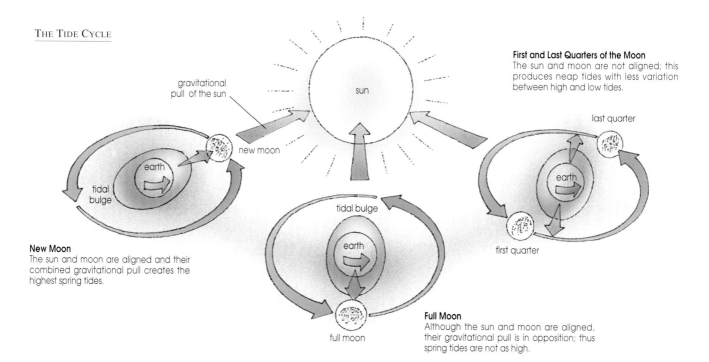

First and Last Quarters of the Moon
The sun and moon are not aligned; this produces neap tides with less variation between high and low tides.

New Moon
The sun and moon are aligned and their combined gravitational pull creates the highest spring tides.

Full Moon
Although the sun and moon are aligned, their gravitational pull is in opposition; thus spring tides are not as high.

TIDES

Divers also need to have a knowledge of tides since tidal movement has a major influence on shore-diving conditions and on the launching of dive boats from the beach. Tides are the rising and falling of the sea according to a pattern determined primarily by the moon and secondarily by the sun. The moon's gravitational pull on the earth results in water in the hemisphere nearest the moon being attracted towards it, while water in the opposite hemisphere bulges outwards from the earth due to **centrifugal force**. The nett effect of these two forces is the 'drawing off' of water across the rest of the earth thereby creating 'ebb' or low tides. As the earth completes one rotation every 24 hours, all regions on earth are influenced by the tide-generating power of the moon and centrifugal force. Thus, all coastal areas should experience both high (flood) tide and low (ebb) tide twice a day (every 12 hours). However, while the earth is rotating on its axis, the moon is revolving around the earth's centre of gravity; but it takes 24 hours and 52 minutes to complete a revolution. Therefore, the time interval between high tide and low tide is actually 12 hours 26 minutes.

The sun, too, exerts gravitational pull on the earth, but to a lesser extent than the moon. Its influence is felt most strongly when the earth, sun and moon are in phase (aligned), as at new and full moon; or when

they are out of phase. When in phase, the solar tide amplifies the lunar tide and this results in higher-than-average **spring** tides. When the sun and moon are out of phase, **neap** tides occur resulting in lower-than-usual tidal changes. Tidal changes are also influenced by the proximity of the moon to the earth. When the moon is in its orbit nearest the earth (at **perigee**), tides are higher; when the moon is farthest from the earth (at **apogee**), tides are lower. When spring tides coincide with a perigee, the highest tides of the year occur. When neap tides coincide with an apogee, the lowest tides of the year occur.

TIDAL CURRENTS

Divers also need to be aware of tidal currents – the horizontal movement of water associated with tides. The direction and strength of tidal currents changes according to tide movements. Water flowing towards the shore as the tide is rising is called a flood tide, and water flowing offshore with a falling tide is called an ebb tide. Tidal currents can become very strong, especially when the water is channelled through narrow areas. Diving in these conditions should only be undertaken by experienced divers and requires careful planning. Divers should always refer to local tide tables and personal evaluations of the tidal status should be made prior to kitting up and again before commencing diving. The dive plan must ensure that there is no need to swim against a strong current at any stage during the dive. Divers should try to plan their dives to coincide with the slack period between tide changes. However, in certain conditions, such as in channels or narrow straits, this period could be limited to only 15 to 20 minutes and this must be taken into account in the dive's planning. Conditions where currents are prevalent lend themselves to drift diving, when divers should take a surface marker buoy (SMB) and have a boat manned by a qualified skipper following them.

SIDEWASH AND LONGSHORE CURRENTS

There are several other types of current that divers must be aware of and know how to handle. **Sidewash**, or **longshore currents**, flow parallel to the shore and are created by waves approaching the shore at an acute angle. The speed of these currents is seldom more than one knot, but it can exceed this depending on wave height, the relative acuteness of the angle and the steepness of the beach. The intensity of the sidewash is greatest inside the surf zone and diminishes with distance from the shore. Longshore currents are likely to wash you down the beach and this must be catered for as you could be swept onto rocks or into an unfavourable exit area. The ability of longshore currents to cut trenches or inshore holes within the surf zone, particularly on steeply sloping beaches, must also be taken into account. Divers wading into the sea down an inclined beach may suddenly find themselves in one of these holes with water over their heads and the longshore current pulling them sideways. Visibility is generally poor as the current will have churned up considerable sediment. The current's effect can also be observed from the movement of sea birds and floating debris. Consideration should be given to aborting the dive if there is a marked longshore current.

RIP CURRENTS

A **rip current**, or rip tide, results from a rule of nature: water must find its own level. Large incoming waves approaching a beach create a surge of water that

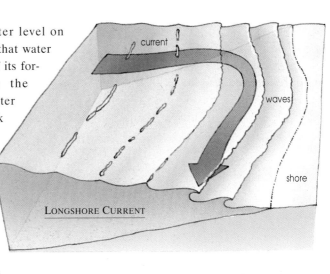

builds up the water level on the incline. Once that water reaches the end of its forward movement the higher level of water must flow back in order to re-establish equilibrium. If it returns through a deeper section of the offshore bottom, forming a type of funnel or valley, then a rip

current is likely to result. The distance that a rip current may flow varies in length from a mere 25m (80ft) to as much as a kilometre (0.6 of a mile) and the current is at its most intense during a lull in wave action. There is also a direct relationship between the size of the surf and the intensity of a rip current – the larger the surf, the stronger the current.

A rip current is made up of three parts: a mouth, neck and head. The mouth is nearest to the shore and is known as the feeder zone. It is fed either by the build-up of water as already explained, by a longshore current or by a combination of both. The neck is where the greatest action is. It is the midpoint of the current and where the greatest velocity is achieved. The head is the area where the rip current finally dissipates its energy and ceases to flow offshore. It is important to be able to identify rip currents as they can be used to advantage, but this should only be attempted by experienced divers.

Rip currents probably account for

LONGSHORE CURRENT

neck

shore

head

mouth

RIP CURRENT   sand bars

TYPES OF RIP CURRENT

Four types are normally identified:

1. Permanent: This occurs where there is a rock channel or fixed substratum valley or funnel. Obstructions such as piers, jetties and pipelines also create permanent rip currents.

2. Fixed: 'Fixed' in this context is a relative term; it could last from a few hours to a couple of months. It is usually caused by a change in the offshore bottom, such as the creation of a hole through supplementary current and wave action.

3. Flash: Flash rip currents are caused by a large surf build-up over a short period of time. They happen suddenly and unexpectedly and disappear equally quickly. Their capriciousness makes them dangerous.

4. Travelling: A travelling rip current is one that is driven along a shore frontage by a strong longshore current. Its occurrence is unpredictable and it may travel over long sections of beach before finally dissipating.

DIVING IN A STRONG CURRENT

1. If diving from a fixed point, start the dive against the current. Stay close to the bottom and conserve energy. Turn back with at least half of your air left and use the current.

2. In strong currents drift diving is the norm. Stay in a group with the divemaster towing a marker buoy. A boat must follow behind to pick you up and in case of an emergency.

3. Avoid free descent; use a weighted descent line or the anchor line.

4. If diving from a boat, there should be a trail line of at least 30m (100ft) so that you have something to hang on to while on the surface.

5. The dive should be terminated while there is still sufficient air for an appropriate decompression stop and for inflating your BC on the surface if necessary. If you should get lost, surface immediately and attract the attention of the boat skipper. Carry a whistle and an inflatable rescue tube or cylinder. A reflective surface, such as a small (unbreakable) mirror is an important item of equipment, as it can be used to attract attention. At night or in low-light conditions, a battery-powered torch or strobe reflecting light attached to your arm is essential for marking your position in relation to a rescue boat or the shore. Waving both hands is a recognized diver distress signal and can be very effective in attracting attention. If unable to attract attention immediately, **do not panic**! Obtain positive buoyancy and wait to be found.

▲ *Excellent visibility and calm seas – ideal diving conditions.*

more beach drownings than any other normal sea condition. Telltale signs of a rip current include: a fan-shaped build-up of water off the beach, a conspicuous stream of dirty water extending into the sea, a foam trail extending beyond the surf zone, and a distinct lack of surf where the current flows outwards. Detection is difficult on windy days.

Using a rip current judiciously, however, will enable the diver to get beyond the surf zone fairly easily. Care should be taken at all times, particularly if the rip current passes through a rocky passage, as a diver could be sucked underwater or scratched by barnacles on the rocks while passing by.

Escape from a rip current is achieved by swimming at right angles to the direction of its flow, in other words, parallel to the beach. Although the current will continue to wash you seaward, you will eventually swim out of its area of influence. Since rip currents are seldom more than 30m (100ft) in width, this is not normally too big a problem.

WIND CURRENTS

Wind currents are generated by strong winds driving the sea's surface layer of water forward. This energy is then transmitted through the different layers of water, with intensity decreasing with depth. Because of the force of the earth's rotation, a current generated through wind action does not flow in precisely the same direction as the wind.

The **Coriolis force** deflects ocean currents to the right in the northern hemisphere and to the left in the southern hemisphere, and is the reason for major currents tending to flow clockwise above the equator and counterclockwise below it. The Coriolis

Convection currents are major ocean currents caused by prevailing wind systems and by temperature differentials between the cold waters surrounding the world's icecaps and the warm waters at the equator. These currents are constant and only vary according to the season. While they have a major impact on the nature of the marine environment, their influence on diving conditions is indirect.

Thermal stratification results from the warming effect of the sun. The sun causes the surface layers of oceans and freshwater systems to rise in temperature. When they are subjected to continuous offshore winds, the warm surface water is, under certain conditions, blown offshore resulting in its replacement by colder, nutrient-laden water from beneath. This rising up of colder water is known as an **upwelling**. Initially the colder water is clear and diving can be very good. However, when the excess nutrients start fostering plankton growth, water clarity degenerates markedly and diving conditions deteriorate.

In static conditions, such as in seas that have been calm for several days, lakes or protected bays and fjords, thermal stratification causes a **thermocline**. This is an area of rapid temperature change – between the epilimnion (the layer of sun-warmed water) and the hypolimnion (the cold, dense, heavier water that accumulates at the bottom).

A **halocline** occurs where sea water meets fresh water from a river. A shimmering effect is created and there is a loss of visibility as fresh water and sea water mix. The freshwater layer is on top as it is lighter than sea water.

force is most effective at higher altitudes and in deeper waters. Current direction varies from approximately 15° with wind blowing on shallow coastal waters to 45° in deep oceans.

The strength of wind-generated currents depends on the velocity of the wind, its constancy and duration. As a general rule of thumb, the velocity of a wind-generated current amounts to 2% of the wind's speed after a 12-hour period of constant velocity. There are, however, three other factors that can influence velocity: the depth of the water; the topography of the sea floor (an irregular floor will create greater drag on the current); and water temperature. Water becomes colder with depth; thus as the temperature decreases, the density or weight of the water increases. It is this extra weight which helps to slow the current down.

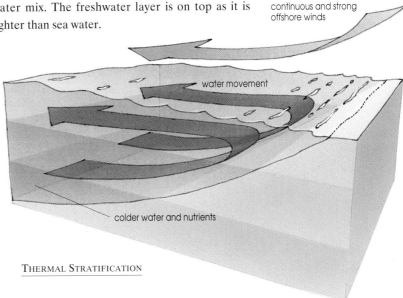

continuous and strong offshore winds

water movement

colder water and nutrients

THERMAL STRATIFICATION

CHAPTER SEVEN

REEFS AND THEIR FASCINATION

R eefs consist of a hardened substratum upon and about which marine fauna and flora gather, and are formed in a number of ways. Rocky reefs, for example, could be the exposed parts of the continental shelf, the remains of calcified sand dunes that became submerged during earlier geological periods in the world's evolution or the result of sudden volcanic action. Coral reefs, on the other hand, are the handiwork of the sea's own creative genius and the story of their birth and growth is an intrinsic part of the fascination of the reef environment. Today, artificial reefs have added a new dimension to reef building as more and more derelict ships are purposely sunk and old car tyres are piled up in barren waters in order to create places where the sea may lay down its carpet of life.

CORAL REEFS

Coral reefs are among Nature's most beautiful yet fragile domains. Found throughout vast areas of the world's tropical and subtropical waters, they vary in size from small underwater patches of coral growth and marine life to Australia's Great Barrier Reef, which, at over 2000km (1240 miles) in length, is the largest living structure in the world. Even in the most unspectacular coral reefs, hundreds if not thousands of different marine species come together to create dynamic ecosystems.

Yellowbar angelfish

Powderblue surgeonfish

Coral reefs are found throughout the world between latitudes of roughly 30°N and 30°S. Current estimates of the extent of coral reefs average around 600,000km^2 (231,600 sq. miles). About 60% of the world's reefs occur in the Indian Ocean and Red Sea; some 25% are found in the Pacific Ocean and the remainder in the Caribbean.

Staghorn coral not only makes a dramatic statement but also provides a place of refuge for fish.

Lipstick tang

Yellow tang

Water temperature and water depth affect the distribution of coral reefs as the small marine organisms that make up the reef's structures require warm water in order to survive. The water temperature should thus not drop below 23°C (73°F) for long; however, corals will not survive in those parts of tropical lagoons which become sun-baked at low tide. Low spring tides also act as a barrier to growth as, despite secreting a protective coating, corals die after prolonged exposure to the air.

Hard corals (also known as stony corals) flourish best at depths above 30m (100ft) although they may still occur to some extent at 40m (130ft) depending on water clarity and availability of light.

LAGOON

BEDROCK FORMED
BY DEAD CORAL

LIFE ON THE REEF

Marine life gathers in abundant and diverse form on a tropical reef. As old corals die out they form the substrate (floor) on which new corals are created, and as the sea washes across the living reef further life is generated in an infinite variety of ways. All occurs in accordance with a dynamic set of rules and relationships developed by Nature at the beginning of time.

1	grasses	11	short coral	21	dolphins
2	starfish	12	staghorn coral	22	moorish idols
3	sponges	13	cornetfish (needlefish)	23	soft coral
4	clown triggerfish	14	butterflyfish	24	grouper
5	parrotfish	15	jellyfish	25	moray eel
6	sea goldies	16	barracuda	26	wobbegong
7	plate coral	17	angelfish	27	sea fan
8	stingray	18	clownfish	28	sea whip
9	brain coral	19	batfish	29	tuna
10	stonefish	20	cardinalfish	30	pelagic shark

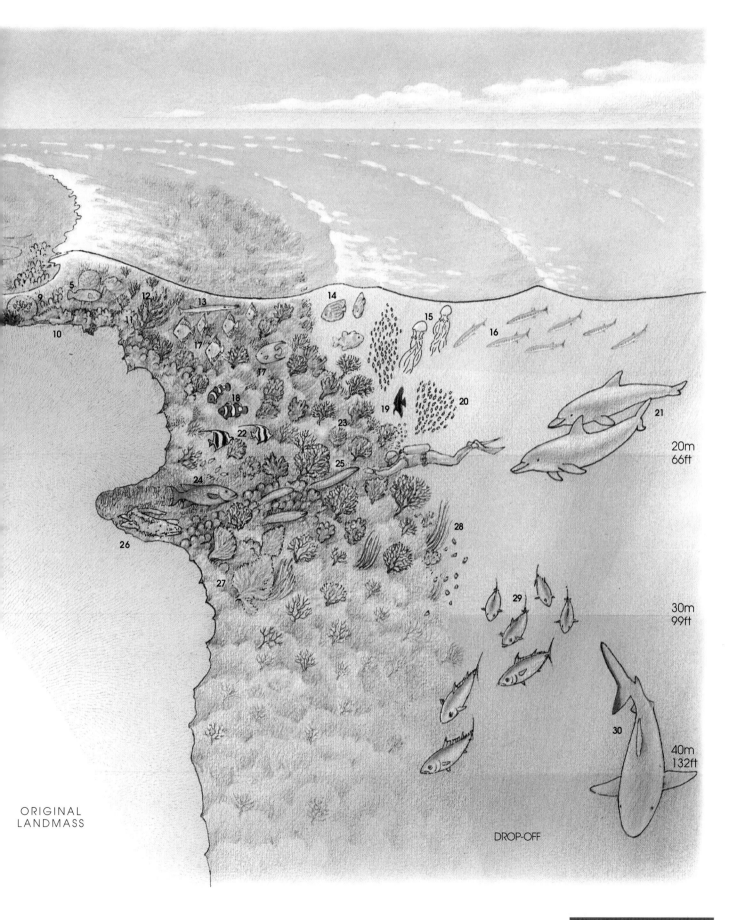

ORIGINAL
LANDMASS

20m
66ft

30m
99ft

40m
132ft

DROP-OFF

Below that depth they rapidly die out and, over time, form solid rock upon which new coral reefs are built. Living hard-coral reefs occur predominantly along the shallow eastern shores of the world's major continents, due to the warm currents generated by the world's prevailing wind systems, and around the small islands and submerged reefs that lie in shallow waters within the current's sweep. Other factors limiting the growth and distribution of coral reefs are water clarity and salinity. Corals cannot survive in waters that carry a heavy silt load or where the salt content in the water is less than 20 parts per thousand (ppt).

Sea goldies, also known as fairy basslets, feed around a feather star.

A CORAL REEF IS BORN

There are four types of coral reef: fringing reefs, barrier reefs, atolls and patch reefs.

Fringing reefs provide a coral fringe which more or less follows the contours of the shore. They are often found along shorelines where the substratum provides a rocky base on which hard corals are able to establish themselves. Because the rocky substratum offers wide spaces on which other sedentary rivals can settle, competition for space is not acute and sponges, soft corals and coralline algae are usually also found in abundance.

THE FORMATION OF AN ATOLL

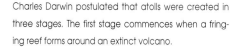

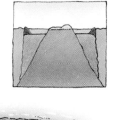

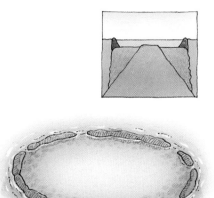

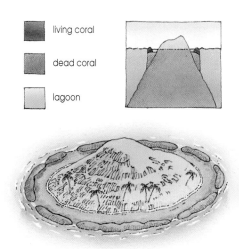

Charles Darwin postulated that atolls were created in three stages. The first stage commences when a fringing reef forms around an extinct volcano.

As the fringing reef expands outwards to become a barrier reef, the island simultaneously begins to diminish in size due to the actions of wind, rain and storms.

Eventually, the island disappears leaving behind a shallow lagoon encircled by a barrier reef. It is at this point that an atoll is said to have formed.

Barrier reefs are substantial structures that often evolve from fringing reefs, but are separated from the shore by a lagoon. (The area between a fringing reef and the shore is the **reef flat**, whereas the area between the barrier reef and the shore is known as the **lagoon**.) Lagoons are fairly shallow, varying from 1m (3ft) to 30m (100ft). The width also varies – from as little as 100m (330ft) to as much as 65km (41 miles) in the case of Australia's Great Barrier Reef.

The lagoon between the barrier reef and land is an area that is often ignored by divers because of the greater colour, life and form of the barrier reef. Its sandy and crushed coral floor may appear drab and lifeless, but divers should not be put off by appearances. Turtles provide an interesting and exciting spectacle as they graze, seeking out the freshest and most nutritious patches of the appropriately named turtle grass, while many species of animals resident along coral reefs often feed, seek refuge, mate or give birth in the lagoon. The juveniles of many reef fish are also to be found in the protected waters of the lagoon before they migrate to the open reefs.

The **atoll** is the third reef type and consists of a circular outer coral reef and a shallow inner lagoon. Atolls are possibly among the most exciting reefs to dive on since their usual remoteness and isolation provide the diver with an unparalleled opportunity to explore and marvel at nature's unspoilt beauty and bounty. Furthermore, because there is no nearby landmass from which silt can bleed into the water and thereby adversely affect the island's ecology, atolls represent one of the most pristine marine environments.

One consequence of this is that the innate fear of humans that fish and many other marine organisms normally display is tempered either by indifference, impish curiosity or defiant territorialism, making atoll diving a truly rewarding experience.

Patch reefs are isolated coral reefs that cling to rocky outcrops or some other form of firm foundation occurring within the required temperature and depth parameters. These reefs are normally fairly flat and can range from a few square metres to many square kilometres in extent.

◄▲ *The diverse shapes and colours of a coral reef provide endless fascination.*

PHYLUM CNIDARIA

REEF-BUILDING CNIDARIA

Hard corals are the primary organisms responsible for the formation of coral reefs. These microscopic animals, known as polyps, are carnivorous and belong to the group (phylum) of invertebrate animals called Cnidaria (previously Coelenterata). Some cnidaria are free-swimming while others are fixed or attached to the reef or substratum. A coral polyp is a sac-like structure with two cell layers – an outer surface or 'skin', known as the ectoderm, and an inner lining to the gut, called the endoderm. The centre of the body consists of a cavity and comprises the gut, which has only a mouth, or orifice, and no anus. The orifice is lined with tentacles which have stinging cells at the top which are used to capture and paralyze prey and to ward off predators (see page 104). The principal diet of coral polyps is zooplankton.

Reef-building cnidarians, or hard corals, deposit limestone cases (skeletons) around and beneath their balloon-shaped bodies to support them and to provide protection for the polyps. The skeletons are known as **corallites**, the walls of which are reinforced by a series of radial partitions known as **septa**; these provide corals with their geometric patterning. Corallites gather to form colonies which characterize the coral's shape and form.

However, only hermatypic corals of the order Scleractina build reefs through their relationship with tiny single-celled algae of the order Dinophyceae. The many different forms and colours within this species are collectively referred to as zooxanthellae. Since coral polyps are transparent, it is the colour of the zooxanthellae within them that gives hard corals the various subtleties of colour they display when healthy. Through photosynthesis the zooxanthellae are able to use sunlight to convert carbon dioxide and water into various sugars and oxygen. This added oxygen is absorbed by the coral polyp thereby increasing its respiration while generating the energy required to drive its life processes. In return, the zooxanthellae gain a home and protection from the coral polyp's limestone case and stinging tentacles.

Gorgeous gorgonian soft corals adorn many reefs.

▶ *A table coral and a sea fan compete for space on a crowded reef.*

However, for this relationship to flourish, the water must be sunlit, shallow and as free of suspension as possible, otherwise photosynthesis will be retarded. (It will not occur below certain depths because of the loss of direct sunlight.) In addition, if the water temperature drops below 20°C (68°F) or rises above 29°C (84°F) the successful deposition of corallite by the coral polyps rapidly decreases. The forces of erosion soon overwhelm those of growth and under these conditions it is not long before the coral reef begins to degenerate and die.

Nature sculpts hard corals into a seemingly endless array of shapes and forms and colours. Within a tropical reef there are corals which are huge and ponderous while others are lace-like, fragile and delicate; some are tiered and overbearing, others are flat and insignificant. Many corals of the same species adopt different shapes in different locations and thus the environment the coral species finds itself in has a great influence on the shape it adopts. In shallow areas where corals are exposed to wave action they are short and squat and often rounded so that they can contend with the forces of water movement. In calmer waters these same species assume more delicate and avant-garde forms, generally as a means of maximizing the amount of light required to generate life-giving photosynthesis. Another factor that helps to determine the shape is competition with other corals for space.

NONREEF-BUILDING CNIDARIA

Nonreef-building corals that occur on coral reefs comprise ahermatypic hard corals, soft corals of the order Alcyonacea Octocorals, gorgonian corals of the order Gorgonacea Octocorals and Pennatulacea, and black corals of the order Antipatharia.

Ahermatypic hard corals are omnipresent as they do not depend on zooxanthellae. Many belong to the family Dendrophylliidae, including the ubiquitous daisy or turret coral *Dendrophyllia* sp. When this coral feeds, its tentacles are extended and its uninteresting turret-like structure is transformed into a bank of bright orange daisy-like flowers. Another ahermatypic hard coral is the dark green, rugged, bush-like *Tubastrea* sp. which can grow up to 2m (6ft) in diameter and in which many dainty tropical fish make their home.

▲ *The open and closed polyps of the turret coral.*

THE SEXUAL LIFE OF CORALS

Although asexual reproduction of corals does occur (when a polyp divides itself and creates an identical daughter polyp), sexual reproduction (when half of the genetic material is provided by one parent and half by the other) is far more common. While most hard corals are hermaphrodite, they avoid incestuous relationships and instead go to a great deal of trouble to fertilize the sex cells of other colonies.

Once a year after a full moon and when spring turns to summer, there is a period of a few days when mating occurs. The build-up to this period takes six months or even longer, during which the eggs of the female hard corals start to develop. At first they are white but as they mature they change colour to vivid shades of pink, red, orange and mauve. At the same time, testes start forming in the male corals, but their spermatozoa develop later since the male matures more quickly. When the conditions are right – the water temperature warm, the tidal variation minimal, the sea calm and the moon still full – the reproduction process moves towards a climax. Half an hour or so before spawning, the eggs and sperm of the respective corals are held at the ready under a thin tissue in the mouth of the polyps. And then, almost as if under some inaudible starter's gun, the polyps release their eggs and sperm in bundles which gently float up to the surface. There, they break open and the sperm swims

off to find an egg of the same coral species. This is a time of intense activity as each sperm cell seeks out a suitable egg to fertilize, but it is also a period of vulnerability since many sea creatures prey on both the eggs and sperm. This is one reason why weather conditions must be right for the fertilization process to occur since settled conditions facilitate mating and also reduce the risk of exposure.

A fertilized egg is known as a planula larva, a tiny creature that is attracted to light and so swims to the surface of the sea where it floats at the mercy of ocean currents and tidal surge. After a period of random floating that can last from a few days to up to two months, the planula sink, hopefully to land on a place where they can settle down to assume the polyp form and to establish a new coral colony. It is almost inevitable that they will have to compete with their neighbours for that precious commodity – space. And so a slow-motion battle commences which the casual visitor may never discern. The extent of the damage can be measured, however, by often sizable pockets of dead corals marking the battleground of two neighbouring coral colonies.

▲ *Coral polyps release their sperm and eggs in bundles.*

When extended, the polyps look like small white flowers. Not all gorgonians are fan-like; some grow as single thin stalks – such as the vivid red coral *Ellisella* and the pale whip coral *Junceella*. These corals tend to favour those parts of the reef which are exposed to prevailing currents.

Sea pens of the order Pennatulacea are soft corals found mainly in sandy areas within or adjacent to coral reefs. They consist of a soft and fleshy unbranched stalk (peduncle) that is anchored to a rock or hard substrate beneath the sand or mud.

Black corals are of the order Antipatharia and although their structures are usually whip-like with some colonies growing to several metres in height, they also occur in branched plant-like colonies resembling trees, ferns and graceful plumes. The coral polyps have six tentacles which cannot be withdrawn. Black corals are not confined to shallow waters because they do not contain zooxanthellae.

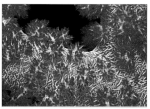

▲ AND ▲ ▲ *Thistle coral has brightly coloured polyps.*

▼ *A sea fan crowned with feather stars in the Maldives.*

Soft corals do not secrete limestone corallites; instead they have disjointed internal skeletons formed from calcareous particles called sclerites. These support the coral, but at the same time allow it to remain soft and flexible. Colonies comprise large numbers of identical polyps connected by soft, fleshy tissue. Each polyp has eight feather-like tentacles which are extended to capture zooplankton and which are concealed when retracted into the polyp's fleshy body. Some soft corals contain zooxanthellae so their distribution on the reef is determined by their access to direct sunlight.

Sea fans and **sea whips** are gorgonian corals belonging to the order Gorgonacea. Sea fans are made up of an array of branches that radiate out in one plane from a central stem, and bear a remarkable likeness to small, flattened trees or to triangular fans. They are made of gorgonin, a horn-like protein substance that is covered with small polyps housed in tiny protruberances, and whose tentacles are used to catch plankton for food.

The skeleton is flexible and either dark brown or black in colour. When dried, it can be cut, shaped and polished; sadly, because of its deep, rich lustre it is exploited for jewellery purposes in some countries.

OTHER CNIDARIA

Besides the hard and soft corals which we have already considered, the phylum Cnidaria also includes jellyfish, anemones and hydroids.

Jellyfish belong to the class Scyphozoa and are bell- or mushroom-shaped creatures with a simple medusa-form body structure and organs that radiate out from a central stomach. Jellyfish swim by pulsing their bodies and jetting water out from beneath the bell. Most are carnivorous, using stinging cells on their tentacles fringing the canopy to stun their prey. Their prey is then passed on to the manubrium or frilly mouth that hangs from the underside of the bell. Jellyfish are an important source of food for the pelagic leatherback turtle.

◀ *Sea pens are anchored to the sea bed by a soft peduncle.*

◀◀ *Anthias and damselfish swim among whip and black coral.*

▼ *The compass jellyfish has a typical medusa form.*

▲ *The anemone's mouth is ringed by tentacles armed with stinging cells.*

THE CORAL POLYP

mouth

tentacles

limestone cup

mesenteries

septa of skeleton between mesenteries

Anemones belong to the order Actiniaria and are solitary fleshy animals that do not have a hard skeleton; instead they are supported by internal water pressure. The body is hollow and cylindrical and is attached to a rock or similar hard surface by a flat adhesive disc. The anemone's mouth is ringed by tentacles armed with stinging cells that are generally harmless to human beings. Tentacles can generally be rapidly retracted to form a protective barrier when the anemone feels threatened; they are also used to capture prey which,

when caught, is killed using the stinging nematocysts in the tentacles and is then stuffed through the mouth into the digestive cavity. Anemones occur in a multitude of colours. In temperate waters they tend to be solitary animals while in tropical waters, the range of species is fewer but they often form large (1m; 40in) flat sheets with hundreds of short tentacles wafting in the current.

An interesting relationship exists between tropical anemones and anemonefishes, or clownfish (subfamily Amphiprioninae), as they are also called. Some 10 species of sea anemone play host to 28 species of these little fish, which use the folds of the anemones' tentacles to hide in whenever they feel threatened. Furthermore, the toxins the anemones use to protect themselves also protect their guests. In turn, the clownfish scavenges for food scraps, algae and parasites within the host anemone's tentacles, helping to keep it clean and healthy. The clownfish's constant movement also creates a respiratory current within the anemone which is good for its general health and well-being. However, while the clownfish apparently cannot survive for long without a host anemone, anemones can thrive without a guest anemonefish. Interestingly, clownfish are

not immune to an anemone's sting. The anemone's mucus contains chemicals to counter the effects of the toxin and thereby overcome the problem of one tentacle stinging another or stinging itself. Clownfish coat themselves with this mucus and so receive the same protection.

Hydroids belong to the class Hydrozoa and comprise a wide range of polyp-covered structures, some feather-like in appearance, some like small trees and others like grasses and seaweed. All form colonies of polyps with a ring of stinging tentacles around the mouth used for defence and for capturing food. Divers should be very wary of hydroids because of their stinging capabilities and their propensity to gather on the metal structures and debris of old shipwrecks.

Bluebottles and other gas-filled hydroids are unusual members of the Hydrozoa class. These specialized hydroids have developed a sac that is inflated with a mixture of nitrogen and carbon monoxide, enabling them to float on the surface of the sea.

Beneath the sac hang long, trailing tentacles which are capable of delivering a powerful sting. One of the best known species of hydroid is the dreaded Portuguese man o'war (*Physalia* sp.) which is blue-green in colour and has a float size reaching 5cm (2in) or more. Its tentacles vary in length, ranging from 30cm (1ft) when fully contracted to 10m (33ft) when fully extended.

These trailing tentacles are inconspicuous against the broken surface of the sea, so it is easy to inadvertently swim into them. Furthermore, they are lined with suckers so they are able to 'cling' to their victim while injecting their poison. The bluebottle's float is shaped in such a way that it either points to the right or to the left. This enables it to 'sail' against the prevailing winds and so avoid being washed ashore. However, when onshore winds exceed an optimum force, this mechanism is no longer sufficient to keep the bluebottles at sea and they are driven ashore, frequently in great numbers.

▲ *The Portuguese man o'war is particularly renowned for its powerful sting.*

▲◀ *The unusual form of a rare Red Sea anemone.*

◀ *Feather hydroids take their name from their distinctive feather-like appearance.*

PHYLUM ECHINODERMATA

The phylum Echinodermata includes starfish, sea urchins, brittlestars, sea cucumbers and feather stars. All are characterized by the spicules or spines in their skins which are developed to varying degrees in the different groups. It is from this that their name is derived: '**ekhinos**', the Greek word for hedgehog and '**derma**', skin. Echinoderms are essentially star-shaped, the protrusions radiating out from a central point (curiously, this radial symmetry is only developed during adulthood). Echinoderms reproduce sexually with both eggs and sperm released simultaneously into the water where fertilization takes place.

The biscuit sea star.

▶ *Feather stars never fail to provide colour and form.*

▼ *This starfish illustrates the 'spiny' nature of echinoderms.*

STARFISH

The echinoderms most familiar to divers are the starfish of the class Asteroidea. These marine animals have a flat body with five or more arms which radiate out like a star from a central axis. Under each arm are small tubefeet which have suckers at the end, providing the means of locomotion. Their principal food sources are detritus or microalgae but some are predators, of which the crown of thorns (*Acanthaster planci*), is notorious for the damage it does to coral reefs. This was first recognized as a serious problem in the 1960s and 1970s when hugely increased populations were observed to be causing serious damage to coral reefs in the Indo-Pacific region, particularly along Australia's Great Barrier Reef and along the coral reefs of southern Japan. Later the threat spread to the islands of Micronesia (particularly Guam) and to the Red Sea.

FEATHER STARS

Feather stars, of the class Crinoidea, are graceful and colourful with small, soft bodies from which 10 or more elongate arms stretch out with elegant symmetry. Each arm, consisting of a central axis with numerous opposite side branches, or **pinnules**, is used to catch food which is then passed to the mouth along hair-lined grooves on the branch's stem. The gut fills most of the body cavity and ends in an anal cone close to the mouth. Crinoids reproduce sexually with the gonads situated in the pinnules of the arms that are closest to the body. The gonads expand steadily just prior to the breeding season and release either eggs or sperm into the water for fertilization. Although crinoids can crawl and even swim in some cases, they are essentially sedentary, using a ring of claw-like segmented limbs situated beneath the body to grip onto the substratum.

THE CROWN OF THORNS

On its own the crown of thorns is a beautiful creature. A fully mature adult measures around 40cm (16in) in diameter and has multiple arms, ranging from nine to 23, which are covered along the dorsal surface with short, fat and formidable spines between 3–5cm (0.8–2in) long. The spines incorporate a sac containing a venom that can cause a skin rash, nausea and severe pain, particularly to those people who are allergic to it. Colours range from orange to a greenish-blue and purple.

The crown of thorns, unlike many other coral predators, does not damage the coral skeleton, but rather feeds on the coral's live tissue. It tends to prefer the polyps of table coral (*Acropora* spp.) and feeds by everting its stomach over the coral so that the digestive enzymes come into direct contact with the coral tissue. In so doing, digestion actually commences before the food enters the starfish's mouth. Its normal pattern of eating is to return to the same coral table until it is dead.

These creatures also tend to aggregate when they feed, due, it is suspected, to attractant chemicals given off during feeding. As a result, their impact on coral reefs is magnified by their concentration in a single area. Normally these giant locusts of the underwater world feed at night and hide deep in cracks and crevices during the day, making their control by the authorities very difficult. Furthermore, they are almost indestructible as they have amazing regenerative powers – a fully functional and developed specimen can regenerate from a portion of one leg!

No definitive answer has yet been found as to why the populations of crown of thorns have suddenly increased. A link was made by some scientists to the steady depletion of the crown of thorns' predators, such as the triton shell which has become popular with collectors, and the reduction in number of pufferfish, triggerfish and humphead wrasse due to net fishing. Other scientists pointed to the effects blast fishing, harbour construction, dredging and pollution have had on the small creatures and coral species which prey on the crown of thorns at the egg and larval stage. Others say that it is a natural cyclical event, pointing to analyses of core samples taken from drillings done on the Great Barrier Reef which indicate that such population explosions have occurred throughout history. They argue that it is only now, as a result of Scuba diving having become such an increasingly popular sport and general awareness of the marine environment improving as a consequence, that this natural phenomenon has been noticed and alarm bells rung.

Injecting them with formalin has proved to be expensive and time-consuming. Other attempts have been made to exterminate them by bringing them ashore en masse and burning them after which the remains are buried. However, scientists are not sure whether the trauma of being caught might not cause them to release sperm and eggs prematurely thus enabling their reproductive cycle to continue. New experiments are being conducted on injecting the animals with swimming-pool acid as this is less expensive than formalin and also possibly more cost effective and efficient than physically removing the animals from the sea. The long-term ecological consequences of the mass destruction of the crown of thorns on the marine environment are still debatable. However, from an ecotourism point of view, their control is vital as few divers will want to dive in reef areas that have been laid waste by this rapacious predator.

▲ *A crown of thorns at work destroying a coral colony.*

BRITTLESTARS

Brittlestars belong to the class Ophiuroidea. They have a flat, circular body from which five or more long thin arms radiate. The arms are jointed and moderately flexible, but they break off easily if force is applied. Brittlestars have a curious form of locomotion with each leg undulating, much like a snake. These marine animals are detritus feeders; the mouth lies underneath the body and has five jaws, each with its own set of teeth. Classified into three groups according to the texture of the body (granular, leathery or covered in spines), they are often colourful and spectacularly marked.

◀ *A striped brittlestar moves by undulating its legs.*

SEA URCHINS

Sea urchins, class Echinoidea, are well known to divers because of their painful spines as well as their distinctive appearance. The sea urchin is encased in a hard calcium carbonate body, known as a **test**. Small tubefeet protrude through tiny pores in the test and provide the sea urchin with its means of locomotion. Protective spines also project through the sea urchin's shell. With certain species these are

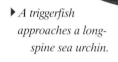

▶ *A triggerfish approaches a long-spine sea urchin.*

▶▶ *An edible sea urchin in a kelp forest off the Scottish coast.*

▼ *Most sea cucumbers look like large slugs but some, like this one in Papua New Guinea, are more spectacular.*

long and mounted on a movable joint, enabling the spine to swivel about and point directly at any threat. Sometimes that threat may come from a diver who may inadvertently stand on the urchin or brush past too closely. Although the prick of an urchin's spine can be painful, it is seldom harmful with the exception of one species, *Toxopneustes pileolus*, which is potentially lethal. Most sea urchins living on rocky shores are grazers, whereas the more flattened sand-dwelling forms feed on detritus.

SEA CUCUMBERS

Sea cucumbers belong to the class Holothuroidea and although they are echinoderms, the cucumber or sausage shape represents a departure from the rest of this phylum. However, their ancient radial symmetry is discernible in the five rows of tubefeet with which they attach themselves to rocks, and the spines in their skin which have been reduced to spicules. Sea cucumbers feed on organic particles which they gather using a series of branching tentacles positioned at the front of the body. Common residents of the reef flats and lagoons of tropical reefs, they vary greatly in colour and pattern. In some oriental countries sea cucumbers are considered to be a delicacy and this has resulted in their being increasingly harvested, often with detrimental effect.

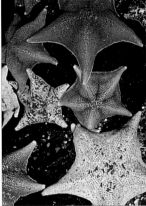

▲ *A group of bat stars
displays vibrant colours.*

◀ *A basket starfish resting on
a sea fan – an unusual and
breathtaking sight.*

PHYLUM CHORDATA

The distinguishing characteristic of this phylum is the existence of a spinal cord or column. Species within the phylum are varied, ranging from simple organisms such as sea squirts to sharks, rays and other fish, frogs, turtles, snakes, whales, and dolphins. Only those classes which divers are likely to encounter on a fairly frequent basis will be discussed.

ASCIDIACEA: SEA SQUIRTS

Ascidians begin their life as tadpole-like creatures with a primitive backbone, nerve cord and tail. As they mature, they lose these features and become **sessile** (immobile and rooted directly by the base without a stalk or peduncle). During metamorphosis the maturing adults synthesize cellulose to produce tests which are surmounted by two turret-shaped siphons. One is for inhaling water and the other for exhaling it once oxygen has been absorbed by blood vessels within the animal's pharynx, and food particles sieved out. The generic common name of 'sea squirts' is derived from their ability to squirt water out of the exhalant siphon. Sea squirts occur in a wide range of forms and colours.

Jacks are fast-swimming predators.

▼ *Powderblue surgeonfishes congregate on a reef at Ari Atoll in the Maldives.*

SUPERCLASS: PISCES

Fish are classified into four major classes: lampreys (Cephalaspidomorphi); hagfish (Pteraspidomorphi); cartilagenous fish (Chondrichthyes); and bony fish (Osteichthyes). Lampreys and hagfishes are primitive fish and only a handful occur worldwide, all in predominantly cold waters. Cartilagenous and bony fish, which are well represented in all seas, are divided into the subclass Elasmobranchii, of which there are a few dozen, and the class Teleostomi of which there are many thousands of species.

Elasmobranchs are usually cylindrical in cross-section (eg: sharks) or flat (eg: rays) and have five to seven gill slits which remain permanently open. Instead of scales they have a tough skin, the texture of sandpaper. Elasmobranchs have an exceptionally well-developed sense of smell which enables them to detect their prey long before seeing it. This factor, together with the fact that certain elasmobranchs (particularly sharks) grow to an enormous size and

are equipped with a combination of formidable strength, powerful jaws and rows of sharp teeth, enables these species to occupy the highest order of the food chain in most marine environments.

Teleosts (bony fish) vary greatly in both size and shape. On each side of the head they have a single gill opening which is protected by a cover that gently opens and closes, fanning water over the surface of the gills. Inside the gills are red filaments which consist of numerous convoluted lamellae containing capillaries at the surface where oxygen diffuses into the blood and carbon dioxide diffuses out. This is a very efficient system since fish can effectively remove about 74% of the available oxygen in a given quantity of water. (Water contains only about 3% of the oxygen contained in an equal volume of air.)

▼ *The waters off Mozambique are a diving mecca offering an endless variety of fish species.*

Elasmobranchs and some teleosts have well-developed electroreceptors which are sensitive to the minute electrical fields produced by all living things. In the case of sharks and rays these receptors, known as the 'ampullae of Lorenzini', are located in pores at the front of the head and enable them to locate prey buried in sediment or where visibility is low. Migratory fish also have electromagnetic sensors so they are able to detect the earth's magnetic field, as well as magnetic anomalies produced by features such as sandbanks or pinnacles which they use for navigation purposes.

REPTILIA: TURTLES

Turtles are relics from the time of the dinosaurs. There is a remarkable degree of compatibility in the types of food eaten and the spatial relationships between the marine turtle species. For example, in the shallow littoral zone the green turtle (*Chelonia mydas*) predominates. It is carnivorous during the first six to 12 months of life, after which it is herbivorous, eating algae and various marine grasses. The hawksbill turtle (*Eretmochelys imbricata*) shares the same part of the shallow littoral zone but also goes deeper, to about 20m (66ft) below the sea's surface, to seek food. It feeds mainly on sponges. Adult loggerhead turtles (*Caretta caretta*) are found principally in the subtidal zone (20–30m [66–100ft] below the surface of the sea) and their principal foods are molluscs, hermit crabs and echinoderms. Olive Ridley turtles (*Lepidochelys olivacea*) are found at the greatest depth, from 30–50m (100–165ft) and feed on crabs and prawns. Leatherback turtles (*Dermochelys coriacea*) are pelagic and feed on bluebottles (*Physalia* sp.), jellyfish medusae and purple storm snails (*Ianthina* sp.).

▲ ▲ *Potato groupers are extremely sociable fish and will often accompany divers.*

▲ *A spotted moray eel is an interesting dive buddy but should be treated with respect.*

▼ *A close-up of the eye and mouth of a balloonfish.*

A MIRACLE OF NAVIGATION

Turtle reproduction is one of Nature's most fascinating dramas. Scientists estimate that turtles are ready to procreate between 10 to 20 years of age. Once gravid, research has revealed that turtles return to the nesting beaches where they themselves were hatched. This astounding ability to navigate accurately underwater, crossing open oceans and travelling vast distances is one of Nature's best kept secrets.

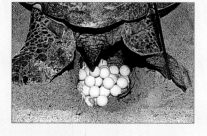

Green turtle hatchling.

Their homing ability requires highly evolved guidance mechanisms which, despite extensive research, are not yet understood. Studies have revealed that turtles have returned to the same beach for 11 separate seasons, and over 90% return to within 5km (3 miles) of their previous nesting site.

A green turtle laying eggs on Pulau Selingan, Malaysia.

Nesting, which is done mainly at night, is a slow and laborious process. At high tide, the gravid turtle emerges from the sea and rests in the wash zone of the beach. She is alert and can easily be disturbed. Once satisfied that there is no danger she advances up the beach well above the high-water mark in order to find a suitable site to lay her eggs. Having found one she commences digging a body cavity with her foreflippers, throwing the sand backwards while gradually moving forwards and

downwards until she has completed a depression, in which she lies with the top of her carapace level with the surrounding beach. Then she carefully digs a cavity with her rear flippers to a depth of between 25–45cm (10–18in) into which she lays her eggs. Eggs are laid in batches; the number per batch varies between species but averages between 100 to 120 eggs per nesting.

Between 50 and 70 days after the eggs have been laid, the hatchlings emerge from their nest in the sand. Once on the surface each hatchling, being about the size of a matchbox, faces the formidable problem of finding the sea, which could be a few hundred metres away. The primary guidance mechanism is believed to be the lighter sky over the water as hatchlings are phototactic, that is, attracted to light. The run to the sea is a time of great risk as the hatchlings are

Hawksbill turtle hatchling.

exposed to the predations of ghost crabs, monitor lizards and birds – and dehydration if they don't reach the water before the sun becomes too hot.

Once the hatchlings reach the sea, the next stage of their life cycle begins. At first they have to deal with the violence of the surf as they make their way through the waves to the open sea. It is another period of danger as they are exposed to predators such as crabs, fish and other organisms. Once in the open sea the hatchlings drift along in the sweep of the prevailing current. All the time their numbers steadily diminish as predators prowl after them. As a result of these and other risks that occur later in their lives it has been estimated that only one to two hatchlings out of every 1000 eggs will eventually reach maturity. After a period of about two years the hatchlings eventually return to coastal waters.

The largest are the leatherback turtles which grow to a length of between 2.5 and 3m (8–10ft) and weigh in excess of 900kg (1985 lb). The relatively thin, heart-shaped carapace of the leatherback has the appearance of dark brown or black leather and bears seven longitudinal ridges. The greatly reduced weight of the carapace, together with the turtle's streamlined shape and long flippers, enables it to swim up to 10kph (6mph) and to cover huge distances while seeking its prey, jellyfish, which are at the mercy of the ocean's currents. Green turtles vary in length from 1.2 to 1.5m (4–5ft), with a maximum mass of 275kg (605 lb). Loggerheads vary in length from 1 to 1.2m (3–4ft) and have an average mass of 160kg (350 lb). Seldom reaching more than a metre (3ft) in length, the hawksbill turtle has a maximum mass of 135kg (300 lb). Smallest of the marine turtles is the olive Ridley. It grows to a maximum of 85cm (33in) with a mass of 46kg (100 lb).

▼ *An encounter with one of the oldest marine inhabitants is something to treasure.*

▲ ▲ *The blue ribbon eel is secretive and is usually seen with only its head protruding.*

▲ *Blue-spotted rays love the sandy areas around reefs.*

◀ *Sea goldies feed primarily on tiny crustaceans and fish eggs.*

▲▲▲ *Eagle rays are found throughout the tropics.*

▲▲ *An emperor angelfish and trumpetfish meet.*

▲ *Collare butterflyfish often congregate in large groups.*

◀ *Black groupers are normally quite diffident.*

◀◀ *Sea goldies typically occur in large groups of females with only a few males.*

▼◀ *The male spinecheek anemonefish is bright red while the female is almost black.*

▼ *Golden butterflyfish usually occur in pairs.*

◀ *Adult oriental sweetlips are found in clear water in the outer lagoon and on the drop-off.*

PHYLUM PORIFERA

SPONGES

Sponges are sedentary animals with neither a mouth and digestive tract nor any of the other conventional organs normally associated with multicelled organisms. The sponge's structure is composed of a few types of cells which together form body tissues that are supported by a skeleton; classification is based on the type of skeleton and the form the spicules take.

A sponge feeds on food particles carried in the water which enter its body through tiny pores dotting its surface. After the water is filtered, it is discharged through large, raised, turret-like openings (**oscula**). The water is pumped through the body by the vibration of many tiny hair-like flagellae which line the body cavity. It is estimated that most sponges circulate their own volume of water every five to 20 seconds and this continues nonstop throughout the day and night.

Sponges, which have a wide range of shapes, colours and patterns, are an important part of the reef's ecology. In addition to being a source of food for a number of marine organisms, they also bore into old dead coral, breaking down its limestone structure. In so doing they create the coral debris that is eventually transformed into sand.

Sponges are multicelled organisms that occur in a variety of forms. Some have amorphous branch structures (▲), some are cup- or goblet-like (▲ ▶), some have long turrets (▶), and others spread themselves across a reef following its contours. Juvenile fish often seek refuge within the nooks and crannies (▶▶).

◀ *The basic sponge structure
consists of vase- or turret-like
bodies joined at the base.*

HUMAN IMPACT ON THE MARINE ENVIRONMENT

The general health of the marine environment is causing increasing concern among the world's conservationists as more and more pressure is placed on it through escalating human population pressures, overexploitation, pollution, soil erosion... to name but a few of the more obvious causes of marine environmental degradation. The long-term costs to humanity are steadily mounting every day.

The felling of trees in river catchment areas, the removal of riverine forests and the draining of wetlands have resulted in increasing soil erosion and the transportation of many millions of tonnes of soil into the sea every year. More and more active reefs become covered in sediment and die each year causing more links in the marine ecological chain to snap.

Pollution of the sea caused by fertilizers washed down by the rivers, industrial and human waste being pumped into it, and petroleum-based filth discharged by passing tankers cleaning their tanks, or from oil rigs and shipwrecks, is affecting marine organisms in many different ways. In the first place, it results in **bioaccumulation**, where pollutants concentrate in the tissue structures of marine organisms as a result of filtering polluted water, feeding on polluted food resources or through passive absorption. In the second place, **biomagnification** occurs when bioaccumulation is passed up through the food chain, with the concentration of the pollutant compound increasing at each level. This is why organisms at the head of a food chain tend to have the highest concentration of pollutants. What the long-term results of biomagnification will be on humankind is still to be calculated.

The leisure industry with which diving is so closely associated is also causing damage to the marine environment. In order to accommodate marinas and boat harbours, coastlines are being altered and shallows dredged. These actions can cause drastic

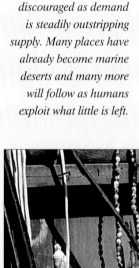

▶AND ▼ The sale of marine specimens as souvenirs should be strongly discouraged as demand is steadily outstripping supply. Many places have already become marine deserts and many more will follow as humans exploit what little is left.

marine environment by commercial fishing must be curtailed and additional reefs will have to be created. Diving is about exploring, studying and enjoying the marine environment; its conservation should be every diver's concern. All litter and extraneous matter should be removed and sound diving techniques practised so that no destruction of any organism takes place. This demands proper buoyancy control; not allowing fins or the water disturbance caused by finning to touch coral reefs; ensuring that gauges, photographic equipment and other items do not make contact with the reef; avoiding holding on to or even touching any marine organism – remember that even just a gentle caress of a polyp could kill it; and demonstrating care and concern about the aquatic world in general. Diving in the shadows of destruction is a stark and depressing experience that fills the soul with a sense of foreboding for the future of humankind. The inevitability of this experience is something all divers should strive determinedly against.

▲ Careless anchoring on coral reefs can cause a great deal of damage.

Sewage outfalls (◀▲) and the dumping of rubbish in the sea (◀) are increasingly becoming problems as the world's population mounts.

variations in the currents that feed nearby reefs, resulting in their slow death. Even more insidious is the international trade in corals, shells, tortoiseshell, live tropical fish, and other fish and marine organisms that are dried and sold to tourists in the countries of origin or exported to other countries and sold to tourists there.

Diving can also impact adversely on the marine environment. An anchor dropped onto coral will destroy that coral, and an anchor chain moving back and forth in the surge of the sea may scythe a path of destruction through a coral forest. Inadequate buoyancy control is likely to result in a diver either bumping into coral, kicking too close to it, or grabbing hold of it and damaging it as a result. In some of the more responsible dive resorts such divers are banned from further diving. As more and more divers take to the underwater world a code of practice will have to be rigidly enforced if nature's fragile reefs are to survive. It is estimated, for example, that over a million divers visit the reefs of the John Pennekamp State Park in Florida annually and this figure is rising.

There is much that is being done, but there is much more that still needs to be done if our marine environments are to survive the present escalating onslaught. Marine parks need to be established on a massive scale. The unending abuse and destruction of the

PHYLUM MOLLUSCA

This phylum is probably the largest of all marine groups. The distinguishing feature is an unsegmented body divided into a head, a visceral mass that includes the digestive and reproductive systems, and a foot. Most molluscs have a radula, a unique tongue-like structure with many rows of tiny teeth which is projected from the mouth and rasps back and forth in order to fragment and scrape up food that is then drawn into the mouth. Nearly all molluscs secrete a calcium shell that covers the body and it is these which shell collectors seek. The phylum is divided into seven classes.

SCAPHOPODA: TUSK SHELLS

This is a small group that is easy to distinguish because of the likeness to miniature elephant tusks. These molluscs have long, tapering, tubular shells, open at both ends, which curve towards the narrow end. The creatures live buried upright in sand or mud with the narrow end, through which water is drawn into the shell, projecting from the sediment surface. The mollusc's foot and mouth are located at the broad end of the shell. The foot is used for burrowing and as an anchor; it also acts as a pump for renewing the water supply within the shell's casing as well as for circulating body fluids. Tusk shells feed on microscopic life forms which are captured by the molluscs' sticky tentacles and then pulled towards the mouth where they are ground up by the radula.

The beautiful spanish dancer is the largest of the nudibranchs.

▼ *Clams are characterized by brightly coloured mantle lobes and a wavy aperture.*

BIVALVIA: BIVALVES

Clams, oysters, scallops and mussels all belong to the class Bivalvia, which is the second largest molluscan class containing nearly 10,000 species worldwide. Species may vary considerably in size – from a mere pinhead to the giant clam, *Tridacna*, which can reach a length of 1.5m (5ft) or more and can weigh as much as 250kg (550lb).

Bivalves are composed of a pair of complementary shell valves hinged together along their backs by an elastic ligament. When threatened, the animal shuts the two valves by stretching the ligament and then, when danger has passed, opens them again by relaxing the ligament. Bivalves have limited mobility

GASTROPODA

The class Gastropoda is the largest in the Mollusca phylum and comprises some 35,000 species. Many gastropods would seem to have little in common (e.g. limpets, cowries and cone shells), but all have the same basic structure (the term 'gastropod' means 'stomach-foot'). The foot, usually large, flattened and brightly coloured, is the most obvious feature. The 'stomach' comprises the remainder of the body, including the heart, nervous and digestive systems, and gills, and is situated on top of the foot within the gastropod's shell. The head, equipped with sensory tentacles and eyes, mouth and radula, is situated at the anterior end of the shell, which is normally the widest part. The radula varies considerably according to species and in some of the more developed gastropods, the mouth is situated at the end of a proboscis.

◀◀ *A flame scallop feels for food with tentacles extended.*

◀ *Chitons are slow-moving creatures adapted to clinging tightly to the rock face.*

▼ *The beautiful tiger spindle cowry rests on a hard coral.*

and usually gather together to form larger colonies, e.g. brown mussels (*Perna perna*). Some bivalves bury themselves in mud or sand, and some burrow into wood and even rock.

Nearly all bivalves are filter-feeders: water is sucked in through a siphon, passed through enlarged sheet-like gills where the food particles are sieved out, and then discharged through an exhalant siphon. Most bivalves reproduce through the discharge of eggs and sperm into the water and fertilization takes place externally. A few species, however, brood their eggs.

POLYPLACOPHORA: CHITONS

Chitons are easily identified by the characteristic overlapping of eight shell plates or valves. These provide the mollusc with protection while still enabling the animal to flex its body and adapt precisely to the irregular rock surfaces to which it clings. Chitons (and limpets) do not cling by suction, but instead secrete a thin layer of slime which creates adhesion. The shell plates are surrounded at their base by a tough flexible girdle which is sometimes armed with protective scales, hairs or spines while the chiton's body has a broad muscular foot rimmed with small gills. This provides the means by which the chiton moves sluggishly about seeking food – mainly algal fronds or diatoms and sporelings which it scrapes from the surface of the rock using its powerful file-like radula.

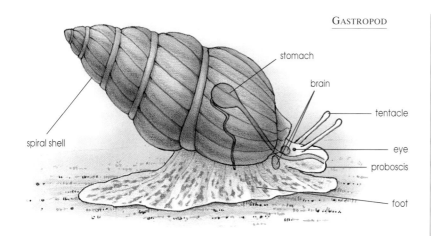

GASTROPOD

spiral shell

stomach

brain

tentacle

eye

proboscis

foot

Another characteristic of gastropods is the spiral form of their shells; however, these may differ substantially. Having said this, not all gastropods have shells! For example, the nudibranchs of the subclass Ophistobranchia are characterized by a reduction or total loss of the shell. In order to protect their exposed soft bodies, they defend themselves by secreting toxic chemicals or re-utilizing stinging cells derived from their prey. They are also brightly coloured which is Nature's way of warning potential predators of their unpleasant taste.

Among some gastropod species there is a distinction in shell size between males and females – the latter usually being the larger. Fertilization is normally external among the more primitive species of gastropods and internal among the more advanced gastropods. With the latter form of reproduction, these species are able to ensure their widespread distribution and long-term survival.

CEPHALOPODA: OCTOPUS, SQUID AND CUTTLEFISH

The cephalopods are probably the most sophisticated of all the invertebrates. During the evolutionary process the animal's head and foot merged and, in the case of octopuses, the primitive outer shell was incorporated within the animal's body while the foot divided into eight or 10 arms equipped with suckers to facilitate locomotion on rocks and the substratum. As the octopus evolved, the mouth moved to a position between the arms and developed a strong beak, enabling it to tear its prey apart. Octopuses also inject a toxin into their prey which, except for the Australian blue-ringed octopus (*Hapalochlaena* spp.), is normally nonlethal to humans. The largest

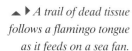 *A trail of dead tissue follows a flamingo tongue as it feeds on a sea fan.*

The colour of the milk conch's stalk eyes distinguish it from other conch species.

invertebrates ever to have evolved in the sea are cephalopods. Some deep-sea squids have bodies 6m (20ft) long and if their tentacles are included their total length reaches 25m (80ft). Squid are the favourite prey of sperm whales, but when a squid of this size is attacked great battles often result.

Cephalopods have mastered buoyancy and, in so doing, have released themselves from the restrictions imposed by a bottom-dwelling life in order to become active swimming hunters. Some achieve buoyancy through the regulation of gases in their internal shells while, in the case of cuttlefish (*Sepia* spp.), the shell has been reduced to an oval flattened plate (cuttlebone) with a texture similar to that of polystyrene. The cuttlebone serves not only as a float but also as a weight, since, through a process of osmosis it is able to regulate the flow of water into and out of the small chambers contained in the cuttlebone, thereby adjusting buoyancy as required.

The cephalopod's means of locomotion is mainly by jet propulsion. The mantle that covers the stomach and gonads forms a sheath which is expanded through muscular action. Water is sucked into the vacuum thus created and then, by contracting the mantle, the water is ejected through a siphon,

◀ *Octopuses, like all cephalo-pods, possess ink glands as a defence against predators.*

▼ *The streamlined shape of the Atlantic oval squid makes it extremely fast.*

thereby creating a jet which propels the cephalopod along, usually backwards. The animal steers itself by pointing the siphon in the appropriate direction.

Mating takes place after an elaborate courtship during which colour change plays a very important role. In prehistoric times the ancestors of squid and cuttlefish dominated the seas and even today the relative abundance of squid makes them a target for commercial fishermen.

SUBCLASS OPISTHOBRANCHIA: SEA SLUGS (SEA HARES AND NUDIBRANCHS)

This subclass is characterized by the reduction or total loss of the animal's shell. Without a shell to protect them, most opisthobranchs secrete toxic chemicals or re-use the stinging cells they derive from their prey (such as anemones and hydroids). In addition, the brightly coloured and patterned nature of nudibranchs warns potential predators of their unpalatability. Some also develop stubby finger-like projections (**cerata**) along their backs which help to provide the animal with a measure of protection. Most opisthobranchs have two rhinophores on the top of their heads which are used as sensory tentacles. Unlike most molluscs, opisthobranchs are

hermaphrodite but they are not capable of self-fertilization and pairs frequently fertilize each other simultaneously. Eggs are laid in long ribbons which are covered with a jelly-like substance and folded into neat rosettes in order to provide protection while they incubate. Once they are ripe they hatch into planktonic larvae.

◀ *A nudibranch rests on a sea squirt off the coast of Borneo.*

PHYLUM BRYOZOA

BRYOZOANS (MOSS OR LACE ANIMALS)

Bryozoans are little known, but not because they are rare or their distribution unbalanced. On the contrary, there are over 4000 species which include some of the most exquisite of all marine animals. The reason for the dearth of knowledge is that most bryozoans do not possess perceptibly distinctive characteristics and resemble a wide range of other organisms. It is from the moss-like appearance of many, but not all, of the species that the phylum name, Bryozoa, meaning 'moss-animal' is derived.

Bryozoans can be broadly classified into four groups according to type: (a) flat-formed species that encrust rocks; (b) flat-formed species that encrust other organisms; (c) upright species with branching colonies that resemble bushes and cactuses; (d) species with calcium skeletons that resemble small coral growths.

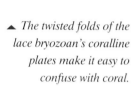

▲ *The twisted folds of the lace bryozoan's coralline plates make it easy to confuse with coral.*

▶ *A nudibranch rests on the arms of a bryozoan.*

ARTIFICIAL REEFS

Artificial reefs, while still in their infancy, are beginning to play an increasingly important role in addressing some of the abuses of the past. These reefs, first developed by fishermen who wanted to increase their yields, are structures that are sunk in order to attract aquatic life. In some countries the creation of artificial reefs has become an industrial process. In Japan, for example, nearly US$1 billion was spent in the period 1981 to 1995 in order to create artificial reefs. Considerable expertise has been developed in the design and construction of **fish aggregating devices** (FADs) which are suitable for the coastal and fishing conditions of that country. The USA has likewise spent millions of dollars on creating artificial reefs, where particular use has been made of waste materials (such as building waste, tyres, vehicles and old ships).

International research has revealed that artificial reefs offer tremendous potential for habitat enhancement. However, what still needs to be determined is exactly **why** artificial reefs attract marine life, **what** form the artificial reef should take and **where** it should be placed. Research done so far tends to indicate that inshore artificial reefs provide feeding, breeding and shelter functions, whereas pelagic artificial reefs primarily provide navigation and feeding functions. It seems, therefore, that localized enhancement of productivity can occur in shallow coastal areas, whereas in the pelagic zone, artificial reefs are more likely to play a concentrating role – certainly as far as fish are concerned.

▲ AND ◄ *The sea's creative genius soon encrusts most foreign objects with a rich variety of marine growth.*

◄ *In some places, however, it takes a little longer for the sea to lay down its carpet of life.*

PHYLUM CRUSTACEA

Crustacea are an advanced group of animals that have evolved a hard external skeleton (or carapace). This provides leverage for the animal's muscles and enables it to act quickly, efficiently and with enhanced power. In order to permit movement, the external skeleton is jointed; this allows for a continuous body cavity and for the elimination of internal repetition of organs, as occurs with segmented worms. External skeletons also make it easier for different regions of the body to become specialized for particular functions and offer effective protection against predators. A crustacean's head acts as a sensory centre and has two pairs of antennae. It also contains a concentration of nerve cells that form a type of limited functioning brain, a cerebral ganglion. The central part of the body – the thorax – houses the reproductive, digestive and excretory organs.

*A colourful
mantis shrimp.*

▲ ▶ *The trade in rock lobsters
as a seafood delicacy is
increasing daily.*

▶ *An almost transparent yet
beautiful shrimp rests on the
tip of an anemone tentacle.*

However, a hard external skeleton prevents continual growth and as a result the crustacean must periodically moult. After shedding an external skeleton that has become too small, the creature swells its body, usually through the intake of water. A new soft carapace is then deposited over the animal's enlarged body and this later hardens to form the new carapace.

Of all the marine animals, crustaceans are said to be the most diverse. In view of this, consideration will only be given to those crustaceans which divers are likely to encounter most frequently.

MACRURA: ROCK LOBSTERS

Rock lobsters, or spiny lobsters, are large, robust crustaceans with a tail ending in a well-developed tail-fan. Both the head and thorax are covered with a single carapace. The rock lobster has 10 thoracic legs, hence the family name 'deca' (ten) and 'poda' (legs), none of which has pincers as they are used for walking only. The growth cycle of the rock lobster is complex and takes almost a year to complete. After mating (the male plasters the undersurface of females with a sperm packet which hardens on contact with sea water and is broken open by the female when she extrudes her eggs), the fertilized eggs are attached to the female's pleopods (the underside of her thorax) and she is then 'in berry'. After about 90 days the eggs hatch into flat spider-like 'naupliosoma' larvae, helpless little creatures barely capable of movement. After nearly eight months at sea, several metamorphoses and numerous moultings, the animal, now in the form of a 'puerulus' larva, miraculously returns to its parental grounds. At this stage it looks like a soft, virtually transparent, miniature rock lobster. After this, the animal matures with moulting taking place at regular intervals as the lobster grows larger.

Rock lobsters are preyed upon predominantly by octopuses, dogsharks and seals, and today are also ruthlessly hunted by man. Lobsters are varied eaters and some species are avid scavengers; their food includes barnacles, mussels and urchins.

STOMATOPODA: MANTIS SHRIMPS

Mantis shrimps have gained their name from their close resemblance to praying mantises. Aggressive animals, they have well-developed second thoracic legs which they use to hunt their prey. They live in holes in sandbanks or under rocks and are intensely competitive and defensive of their territory against others of their kind.

STENOPODIDEA: CLEANER SHRIMPS

Cleaner shrimps are similar to swimming prawns (Penaeidea) except that they are brightly coloured and possess large nippers on the third pair of walking legs. The cleaner shrimp (*Stenopus hispidus*), for example, is very colourful with red and white banded legs and body. These animals provide a useful service to the fish community as they remove parasites and bacterial growths from the surface of fish, helping to keep them healthy. Their vivid colours make it easier for the fish to recognize cleaner shrimps, and because of the general use of colour as a means of defence in the underwater world and the useful function that these animals fulfil, they are not preyed upon by their clients.

▲ *Cleaner shrimps are seen here at work on a grouper.*

◀▲ *The violet-spotted lobster is a conspicuous reef dweller.*

MARINE PLANT LIFE

It is not intended to deal with the different forms of underwater plant life in any detail as this is a vast and complex study that lies beyond the scope of the book. Reference will only be made to the plant divisions and their characteristics.

Seaweeds are separated into three divisions:
Chlorophyta or green algae
Phaeophyta or brown algae
Rhodophyta or red algae

Chlorophyta has an overriding green colour due to the high chlorophyll content. Green algae have three basic body forms. The first is the order Ulotricales which consists mainly of flat sheets that vary from one to two cells thick. The second is the order Cladophorales which consists of filaments of cells placed end to end; and the third is the order Siphonales which consists of tubes grouped together to form complex plant bodies.

The **Phaeophyta** contains a wide variety of plant forms including membranous forking plants, cushions, simple fans and complex tree-like forms such as the kelps which occur in certain cold waters.

The **Rhodophyta** is the most comprehensive and largest marine plant division. Rhodophyta seaweeds contain predominantly red and blue pigments, thus the majority of plants are either red or purple or a combination of the two. However, some also contain chlorophyll and are thus green in colour and easily confused with plants belonging to the Chlorophyta or Phaeophyta divisions. Many Rhodophyta species found in the intertidal zone are tough, wiry and have many branches so that they can withstand wave action. These tend to be green to red or reddish-brown. Most deep-water forms are purplish-red as their phycobylins absorb the blue-green light rays that penetrate deepest in water; the energy absorbed from this light is transferred to the chlorophyll for photosynthesis. Most deep-water algae form flat sheets as this allows them to absorb the maximum amount of sunlight.

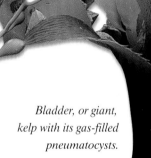

Bladder, or giant, kelp with its gas-filled pneumatocysts.

▶ *Kelp grows quickly and dense forests develop, which nature thins out regularly during violent storms.*

▲ *One should swim carefully through a kelp forest to avoid being snared.*

GLOBAL WARMING AND THE MARINE ENVIRONMENT

The earth is surrounded by its own atmosphere which acts as an invisible blanket keeping essential heat from escaping into the atmosphere. Short-wave energy from the sun passes through the atmosphere and strikes the earth; much of it 'bounces' off and returns to the atmosphere as long-wave radiation. In the atmosphere there are a number of gases (carbon dioxide, methane, nitrous oxide and water vapour) which absorb and trap this long-wave radiation and in so doing create an 'atmospheric greenhouse'. Without this, the planet would be plunged into a massive Ice Age. However, as man pumps ever greater amounts of greenhouse gases into the atmosphere, notably carbon dioxide which is released in colossal quantities through the burning of fossil fuels and trees, together with a wide variety of industrial gases, the greenhouse effect is increased and more and more long-wave radiation is trapped. The result is that the earth is steadily warming and this is having an adverse effect on climatic systems. Furthermore, some of these gases, namely the chlorofluorocarbons, are eroding the protective ozone layer in the atmosphere resulting in the destruction of our protection against ultraviolet radiation and an increase in cancer among humans.

Coral reefs have two important beneficial influences as far as the greenhouse effect is concerned. Firstly, carbon dioxide, the major greenhouse gas, dissolves in the sea and creates a very diluted form of carbonic acid. Coral reefs, as well as many other shell-building marine animals (particularly plankton), require carbonic acid in order to build up their limestone cases; therefore, through the absorption of carbonic acid during their growth they are able to provide a buffer against excessive acid production and, in turn, reduce carbon dioxide levels in the atmosphere. However, should these carbon dioxide levels become excessive, carbonic acid levels in the oceans of the world will increase accordingly, eventually overwhelming the shell-depositing marine creatures. As acidity levels rise, the strength of the carbonic acid in the sea will intensify and the shells of the plankton and the limestone cases locked into the coral reefs will steadily dissolve. This, in turn, will add considerably to the acidity of the sea. Nature's delicate balance will be disturbed and the disastrous consequences of this will snowball as element after element in the marine environment collapses.

Coral reefs also play an important role in protecting the land against the surges of the sea. With the greenhouse effect causing temperatures on the planet to increase, the earth's polar icecaps may melt and sea levels will rise. This will result in low-lying areas being submerged and, where coral reefs have been removed or killed off, the effect on the unprotected coastline will be catastrophic.

Another important service that coral reefs fulfil is helping to keep the sea's salt concentrations constant. Rivers pour vast quantities of minerals and salts into the sea on a daily basis and yet the chemical composition of the sea's water remains remarkably consistent.

Coral reefs are believed to play an important role in balancing the chemical equation through the steady conversion of coral reef flats and shallow lagoons into large evaporation pans where sea water is captured and the salt is crystallized out. If the level of the sea rises, it is almost inevitable that these evaporation pans will become inundated and vast concentrations of salt will be leached back into the sea, further exacerbating the growing imbalance in nature. What the implications of this will be on the marine environment and on humankind is difficult to calculate.

CHAPTER EIGHT

DANGEROUS MARINE ORGANISMS

An enormous number of marine organisms are harmless and the diver can move among them with complete ease. However, it is important for divers to be aware of those organisms which are dangerous and to be informed about relevant first aid procedures.

Dangerous marine organisms can be divided into those that inflict physical injury, sting, infect, or poison. This book will concentrate on those species that inflict physical injury or sting as these have a direct bearing on diver behaviour.

Those that infect or poison generally result from water contamination or from eating poisonous marine animals and organisms and are thus not directly diving related.

MARINE ANIMALS THAT INFLICT PHYSICAL INJURY

Marine animals that cause trauma are without a doubt the best known and most feared form of danger in the marine environment. Outstanding among these are sharks. There are, however, numerous other marine animals that can cause physical injury to divers, including electric rays, eels, octopuses and various fish.

Lionfish

SHARKS

Sharks, whose ancestry goes back to the days of the dinosaurs, have come to be both revered and loathed, respected and feared, admired and hated… but never ignored. At first, divers were paranoid about sharks; they were seen as enemy number one and their destruction was encouraged. Gradually,

The reef whitetip shark is normally docile but may become aggressive around speared fish.

however, a growing admiration for these fearsome and chillingly beautiful creatures began to take root, and today the camera is increasingly taking the place of the speargun and other instruments of death.

There are some 350 species of shark worldwide, of which approximately 10% are known to have the capability to attack human beings.

Probably the most notorious of all sharks is the **blue pointer**, also known as the **white pointer**, **white death**, and **great white** (*Carcharodon carcharias*). This member of the Lamnidae family is the epitome of the man-eating shark. An adult grows to a length of up to 6.5m (21ft) and can weigh up to

Palette surgeonfish

▲ *Photographing the great white is certainly not for the fainthearted!*

▲ *The distinctive shape of the hammerhead shark makes for easy identification.*

2 tonnes. Unpredictable and fearless with large jaws and huge triangular-shaped serrated teeth, they are fearsome creatures in every respect. Their bite force is estimated to be about one tonne per cm^2 and with this brute force and stength, they often propel their victims right out of the water! Blue pointers are usually found in cold waters where there are large seal and sea lion populations.

The **oceanic whitetip** (*Carcharhinus longimanus*) has been described as the most dangerous of all sharks. A large stocky shark (adults vary in length from 1.7 to 3m; 5ft 6in to 10ft), it has distinctive long, rounded, whitetipped pectoral fins. Fortunately, it prefers deep open water and is seldom seen in water shallower than 40m (130ft). It has

gained much of its notoriety from its habit of congregating around mid-ocean disasters such as shipwrecks and plane crashes. Occasionally it can be seen swimming leisurely, breaking the surface with its high white-mottled dorsal fin. The oceanic whitetip is known to become very aggressive, particularly if there is food about. It has a grey-bronze upper body and white underside, and large broad teeth which are deeply serrated. Birds, pelagic fish, octopus, turtles and carrion all form part of its diet.

Bull, or **Zambezi** sharks (*Carcharhinus leucas*), are circumglobal predators often found in estuaries, sometimes many miles upstream where the water is no longer saline. Robust and dangerous, this grey shark should be treated with great caution as many attacks on humans have been attributed to it. It has no distinctive markings, but has a high dorsal fin and broad triangular saw-edged upper teeth. It feeds mainly on small sharks, fishes and dolphins.

Tiger sharks (*Galeocerdo cuvieri*) are voracious predators on fish, birds, mammals and turtles and have also been implicated in many attacks on humans. They grow up to 5.5m (18ft) in length and weigh up to 560kg (1235lb). The tiger shark has large saw-edged cockscomb teeth.

Damage done by sharks to their human victims varies. In some cases only abrasive lesions of the skin are inflicted, usually resulting from the shark rubbing its intended victim prior to attack. It is believed that this indicates that the shark is uncertain about the nature of its prey. Bite injuries usually comprise either linear concentric slashes where the teeth of the upper jaw have raked the victim, or puncture wounds from both jaws encircling the victim's body. These marks typically indicate that the shark released its victim after the first bite – 'bite and spit' behaviour occurs with most species and presumably indicates that the shark found the victim unsuitable. When genuine feeding attacks occur, wounds are ragged. In most recorded cases there has been a single bite, although multiple bite attacks have occurred resulting in extensive body wounds. If the victim is not killed immediately, death often follows shortly thereafter from massive haemorrhaging and shock. Having attacked once, the shark rarely attacks other people in the area but concentrates single-mindedly on its victim.

MINIMIZING THE RISK OF SHARK ATTACK

1. Treat all sharks with the utmost respect. While some are harmless and docile, others are not – don't rely on your ability to distinguish between them.

2. Don't dive with an open wound and don't dive where fishermen are cleaning their catches.

3. Avoid dirty water and water with poor visibility. Not only does this impair your vision and ability to take evasive action, but many sharks are attracted to this sort of water because of the likelihood of finding food.

4. Always dive with a buddy and stay close together. Research has revealed that sharks tend to attack people who are on their own or some distance away from others. Avoid long periods on the surface in open water where sharks have been known to attack.

5. Be careful at dusk when sharks feed and are known to be particularly active.

6. If sharks become inquisitive and bold it is better to get out of the water, even if your nerves can stand their close attention. If possible keep your back against the rocks and go to the surface back-to-back with your buddy.

7. Be calm, at least on the outside and in your movements! A shark may mistake quick movements for those of a struggling fish, in other words, an easy meal. Remember sharks have poor eyesight and are attracted by movement and smell. There is little you can do about smell, but there is when it comes to movement, so move cautiously.

8. Never tether fish or abalone near the body.

9. Should a shark's behaviour become threatening, it is important to try and break its attack cycle. Back away steadily, avoiding sudden movement, and get to a rock face or overhang as quickly as possible. Should you fail to reduce the shark's attention and the situation begins to look ugly, remember that a shark's snout is sensitive and therefore a sharp blow on it with a knife or shark billy (should you have one), or even your fist plus a shrill scream are likely to break its attack cycle and, by rights, it should then leave you alone. These tactics, however, should only be used as a last resort, as they could make the shark more aggressive, particularly if it is a great white.

▲ *Ragged-tooth sharks will become dangerous if provoked.*

HOW TO TREAT A SHARK BITE

1. Remove the victim from the water and lay him or her on the beach just out of the tide's reach so that the head is lowermost. Don't waste time going any further up the beach.

2. Begin treatment at once; do not immediately rush the victim to hospital.

3. Maintain your calm and that of those around you, and reassure the patient.

4. Start by stopping the bleeding, applying direct pressure above or on the bleeding artery. If clamps are available, use them to close severed or damaged arteries. A tourniquet should only be applied if the leg or arm has already been severed or if the damage is so severe that amputation is likely. (If a limb is deprived of blood for any length of time, gangrene is likely to set in making amputation inevitable; every effort must be made to ensure maximum blood circulation at all times.) If bandages are used, it is important to see that they are used to stop the bleeding and not merely to cover up the wound.

5. Place a towel or light clothing over the patient. If he or she is wearing a wet suit, do not remove it as this will create too much movement. The wet suit may also help to keep the victim warm and reduce shock while keeping organs and tissue in place.

6. Send for an ambulance and medical personnel. Inform ambulance control of the extent of the injuries in as much detail as you can so that they can despatch a suitably qualified crew with the appropriate medical equipment. Do not move the patient without expert supervision.

7. Do not give the victim anything by mouth.

ELECTRIC RAYS

Electric rays belong to the family Torpedinidae and are the underwater world's hovercraft. They are rather slow fish whose pectoral fins have been extended into wing-like structures, resulting in some species looking like very large dishes onto which a tail has been attached. Most lie semi-submerged in mud or sand at shallow depths where they feed mainly on crustaceans.

Electric rays discharge a current varying from 8 to 220 volts between the electrically negative ventral side of the body to the electrically positive dorsal side. This discharge occurs whenever the fish's electric organs, situated on either side of its eyes, are touched. Shocks can vary from a pricking sensation to serious shocks that may cause temporary disablement, leading to possible drowning.

First Aid

There is no specific treatment.

▲ ▶ *The electric organs of the ray can deliver a nasty shock.*

▶ *The great white probably has the greatest bite force of any creature in the world.*

▲ *The amiable moray eel (left) is more often seen than the conger eel (right), which can be vicious.*

◄ *Moray eels can become very affectionate but be careful!*

EELS

Eels known to have displayed aggression towards humans belong to the family Murenidae, of which *Gymnothorax melaegris* and *G. nudivomer* are possibly the most aggressive. The giant moray (*G. javanicus*) is capable of inflicting severe injury but it is a normally docile and lovable creature. The conger eel (*Conger labiatus*, family Leptocephalidae) is also considered to be dangerous.

Moray eels have a fearsome appearance underwater but their aggressive-looking posture as they open and close their mouths is actually only respiration. While a number of morays have been tamed and obviously welcome the attention and the tasty morsels of food they receive, it is **not** recommended to feed these fish as they will begin to expect it from all divers. You may be fortunate but the divers following you may be attacked by the eel looking for food. Nature has armed them with three sets of teeth that can dig deep into a diver's body; their muscular jaws clamp down with great power and because of their slippery bodies they are awkward to grasp. Equally, if they are in their holes they are almost impossible to dislodge and so the diver has little choice but to rip free from the eel's grasp. Wounds are usually of a torn and ragged nature and profuse bleeding is typical.

First Aid

1. Wash the wound thoroughly; depending on its severity, stitches may be required.
2. Bites often turn septic so antibiotics and anti-tetanus may be needed.
3. Monitor carefully for any sign of deterioration.

◄ *If approached cautiously, morays may come out to greet you.*

The blue-ringed octopus is small but dangerous.

Triggerfish can often become aggressive when guarding their nests.

OCTOPUSES

Octopuses feed predominantly on shellfish and have a sharp beak to enable them to crush the shell of their prey. A bite from an octopus can thus be painful but, in addition, venom from their salivary glands may be injected into the wound; the venom contains enzymes which cause inflammation, gross swelling and numbness. The condition could last for a couple of hours or go on for a few days.

The blue-ringed octopus (*Hapalochlaena maculosa, H. lunulata*) is the most dangerous of all the octopods. It is a small creature in comparison to its cousins – with its tentacles extended it varies in size from 2cm (0.75in) to 20cm (8in). Occurring in the Indo-Pacific region, predominantly in Australia and to a lesser extent in New Zealand, Papua New Guinea, Indonesia, Fiji and Japan, it hides in old shells and at low tide can be found in rock pools, often within clumps of sea squirts. It is yellowish-brown in colour with ringed markings on its tentacles and striations on its body. These markings turn a beautiful iridescent blue colour when the animal is disturbed and becomes angry or excited. Although attractive, it is highly venomous and must be treated with absolute caution.

Its normal hunting tactic is to bite into a crustacean's back while holding it with its tentacles and then to paralyze it with venom. Sometimes it may swim over its prey and squirt toxic saliva into the surrounding water. The prey soon becomes disoriented and after a little while dies, to be consumed later at the octopus's leisure.

A bite may go unnoticed for 15 minutes or so after which an area of about 1cm (0.4in) in diameter goes white and becomes very swollen. Soon the victim's mouth, neck and head becomes numb and nausea develops. Vision becomes blurred and doubled, speech is slurred, while swallowing and breathing become increasingly difficult. This condition soon leads to paralysis, which may be partial to begin with but may subsequently develop into a general paralysis, resulting in death.

First Aid

Before paralysis sets in:
1. Wash the wound out thoroughly with any fluid or antiseptic available.
2. Immobilize the affected limb and bandage the wound tightly.
3. Keep the victim rested, lying on his or her side in case of vomiting.
4. Make immediate arrangements for emergency medical support.

After paralysis has set in:
1. Apply mouth-to-mouth respiration and make sure that the victim does not start to go blue. Keep the airway clear, remove any obstructions. Keep the procedure up until the victim is hospitalized.
2. Apply external cardiac massage, if necessary.
3. Keep reassuring the victim, who can hear but cannot communicate.
4. Do not leave the patient until an ambulance or other medical assistance has taken over.

SURGEONFISH

Surgeonfish are very beautiful, brightly coloured, smallish tropical and subtropical reef fish. They represent absolutely no threat to divers until they feel cornered or threatened. When this happens, these intrepid little fish may attack, using the razor-sharp blade-like spines that occur on either side of the body near the tail as weapons. The fish thrashes its tail against the enemy as it attacks and the spines can cause deep lacerations. It is from these scalpel-like spines that the surgeonfish gets its name.

First Aid

The diver must abort the dive and have the injury treated immediately. Care must be taken to wash the wound out thoroughly with the hottest water possible in order to help neutralize the effect of possible toxins. Bleeding must be stopped and the wound treated with antiseptic ointment.

TRIGGERFISH

Triggerfish (of the family Balistidae) lay eggs in sandy depressions within coral reefs. Large male triggerfish guard the nest and may attack divers who come too close. Their teeth are very strong, and can go through rubber fins and 4mm (0.16in) wet suits without difficulty, drawing blood in the process.

First Aid

Clean the wound thoroughly with hot water and treat it with an antiseptic cream.

▲ *The aggressively territorial Sohal surgeonfish can inflict a nasty cut.*

VENOMOUS MARINE ANIMALS

There are more than 1000 species of fish that are either poisonous to eat or venomous. These are some of the ones that are dangerous to divers.

STONEFISH

These fish belong to the family Scorpaenidae and the dangerous species are: *Synanceia verrucosa, S. trachynis* and *S. horrida*. Growing to a length of about 30cm (12in), they occur throughout the whole of the tropical Indo-Pacific region and are probably the most dangerous of all fish. Their danger lies in two directions – firstly, the ferocity of their venom which is injected into the victim through one or more of 13 dorsal spines capable of piercing through even the toughest rubber sandshoe; and secondly, their dormant disposition. They lie in sand, mud or coral debris with only their eyes showing so it is easy to tread or put your hand on one of them.

Pain is immediate and increases in intensity for 10 minutes or so until it becomes excruciating. It can cause delirium or unconsciousness resulting in drowning. Cardiovascular collapse is not uncommon.

First Aid

1. The patient must be laid down and kept calm. Extract any spines and wash the wound. Keep the affected area elevated as much as possible.

2. The wound should then be immersed in the hottest water the patient can stand – at least 50°C (122°F) – in order to break down the toxins. If this is not possible, then hot packs should be used. Burning cigarette ends have also been used as an alternative. The affected area should be washed constantly.

3. In the case of a loss of consciousness, apply external cardiac massage and mouth-to-mouth respiration. Continue until resuscitation is complete or death is confirmed.

4. Get medical help to the patient as quickly as possible. Stonefish antivenin is available in Australia and good results have also been achieved with treatments such as an injection of hyoscine butylbromide or emetine hydrochloride into the wound. These should be administered as soon as possible.

SCORPIONFISH

There are some 330 scorpionfish belonging to the family Scorpaenidae, some of which are extremely venomous. Like stonefish, they have dorsal spines which are used primarily as a means of defence by injecting poison into their adversaries – which could be your foot or hand should you inadvertently put either in the wrong place! Distribution is widespread throughout tropical, subtropical and temperate regions. Some are fairy-like fish that glide gracefully by with flowing feathers and butterfly wings, others are grotesque and ghoulish with scraggy heads and camouflaged bodies. Generally scorpionfish take on the colours of their environment and so are able to remain well hidden and lie in wait for their prey.

First Aid

Same as for stonefish (above).

▼ *Stonefish are considered to be the most venomous of all fish.*

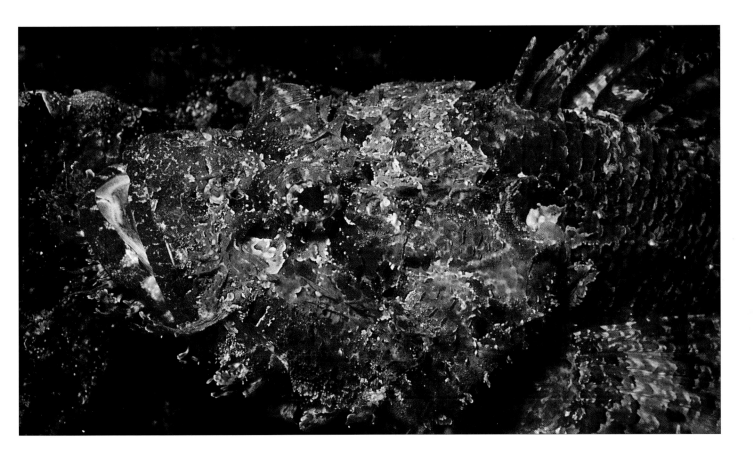

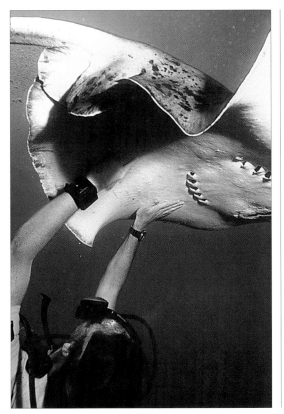

STINGRAYS

Stingrays belong to the family Dasyatidae and are bottom-dwellers, their large flat bodies often submerged in sand with only their eyes visible.

As with electric rays, stingrays are not aggressive, but if provoked (eg: unwittingly stood upon) or threatened they can become vicious. They use their tails as deadly whips, swinging them upward and forward in a reflex action which can produce sword-like lacerations. At the base of their tails they also have one or more venomous spines which may be used as a means of defence independently of the tail or in concert with it. Stingray attacks can be vicious and are sometimes fatal – death coming either from damage done by the tail, from the venom injected by the spines or from both.

First Aid

For injuries caused by the stingray's venomous spines, the same treatment as for stonefish should be administered. In the case of lacerations caused by the tail, attention should be paid to stemming the loss of blood and treating for shock.

▲ *Scorpionfish blend in with their environment.*

◀ *Stroking stingrays should be avoided – for the sake of the diver as well as the animal.*

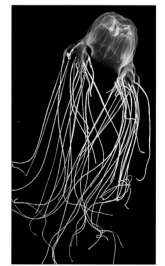

Stinging hydroids – graceful flowers of the sea but not to be touched.

▼ *The box jellyfish, or sea wasp, has tentacles that can reach 3m (10ft) in length.*

VENOMOUS CNIDARIA

This phylum contains some 9000 species and classification is difficult, since it contains members that are grossly dissimilar in appearance and mobility. Species range from reef-building invertebrates to anemones, from jellyfish to hydroids. The one factor common to all is their basic polyp structure and the development of nematocysts or stinging cells on the animal's tentacles. These either adhere to the animal's prey, by means of a sticky mucus or a coiled spring, or develop minute needles which penetrate the prey and discharge venom. The function of the nematocyst is to incapacitate and retain its prey.

Distinction can be made between mobile and immobile classes of Cnidaria. Species included in the former are the Portuguese man o'war (*Physalia* sp.), the sea wasp or box jellyfish (*Chironex fleckeri*), the jimble (*Carybdea rastoni*), various other sea wasp varieties (*Chiropsalmus* spp., *Carybdea* spp., *Tamoya* spp.), the mauve stinger (*Pelagia noctiluca*), and various blubber jellyfish (*Catostylus mosaicus*, *Rhizostoma cuvieri*, *R. pulmo*). Immobile species

include fire coral (*Millepora* spp.); sea anemones (*Actinia* spp., *Actinodendron* spp., *Alicia* spp., *Anemonia* spp., *Calliactis* spp., *Lebrunia* spp., *Physobrachia* spp., *Rhodactis* spp., *Sagartia* spp., and *Telmatactis* spp.); and stinging hydroids (*Aglaophenia* spp., *Lytocarpus* spp.).

Stings from venomous Cnidaria range from a mild itch to a throbbing and burning pain that develops over 10 or more minutes. Severe blistering and even necrotic ulcers may also result. Fevers may develop, while respiratory distress and occasionally cardiovascular failure may occur.

The intensity and nature of the manifestations vary according to the species involved. The sting of the sea wasp (*Chironex fleckeri*) is often lethal and has claimed more lives in Australia than have sharks, while that of many anemones may be imperceptible because the nematocyst is incapable of penetrating deep enough into the skin.

The maturity of the animal also has a bearing on its potency and the effect of the toxin is influenced by the body weight of the victim (stings are usually worse with children). The thickness of the victim's skin at the point of contact, the physical fitness of the victim and the existence of allergies all influence the consequences of a cnidarian sting.

First Aid

1. The victim must be assisted from the water (rescued if necessary) and made to lie down. Keep the victim as calm as possible.

2. Resuscitation must be applied if needed. Arrange for a doctor and emergency services to be called. Because of the potency of the box jellyfish sting it is imperative that professional medical treatment be sought as quickly as possible.

3. The wound area must be carefully inspected and all traces of the offending animal removed.

4. Care must be taken to avoid triggering off any more nematocysts by dousing the area liberally with vinegar and using tweezers to remove any remaining nematocysts.

4. Often local remedies work remarkably effectively with less serious cases. As mentioned above, a mild acetic acid, such as vinegar, helps to reduce the number of nematocyst discharges. Paw paw (papaya), calamine lotion, ammonia and lime juice can also be used, often to good effect, to relieve the pain of milder stings.

OTHER VENOMOUS MARINE ANIMALS

There are a number of other marine animals whose sting divers must endeavour to avoid; some of the most important are the following:

SEA SNAKES

There are some 50 species of sea snake worldwide, of these the yellow-bellied sea snake (*Pelamis platurus*) and various species of banded sea snake (*Laticauda* spp.) are considered to be particularly dangerous to human beings. Sea snakes are found predominantly in the Indo-Pacific region and throughout Asia. They are not found in the Atlantic. Bottom-feeders, such as the *Laticauda*, which have the ability to dive to 100m (330ft) in pursuit of prey, are restricted to shallower coastal waters where they breed and lay their eggs on the shore, in caves and crevices. They can survive for long periods out of water. Pelagics, such as the yellow-bellied sea snake, are surface feeders and drift with warm-water tides. Breeding and birth takes place at sea and these snakes tend to congregate into packs. They cannot survive for long out of water.

Sea snakes have adapted to marine conditions by increasing their lung capacity while simultaneously decreasing their metabolic rate and developing an increased tolerance for low oxygen levels. As a result, a sea snake can remain submerged for up to two hours at a time. It has also developed flaps which seal off its nostrils while underwater and the tail has been flattened to form a paddle used for propulsion. Sea snakes are inquisitive and occasionally aggressive, but usually only if threatened. Although their venom is extremely toxic, the apparatus for delivering venom is not well developed and researchers estimate that only about 25% of human bite victims ever show any signs of poisoning.

A person bitten by a sea snake may display no symptoms for several hours. The first indication is an awareness of feeling 'different' which ranges from euphoria to restlessness and depression. This is generally followed by a drying of the throat and nausea. In due course, a feeling of weakness gradually changes into paralysis. Lockjaw and drooping of the eyelids are characteristic of a sea-snake bite.

▼ *The banded sea snake may be beautiful but it is known to be dangerous to humans.*

First Aid

1. Remove surface venom, but keep it for identification purposes. (If possible, try to retain the snake.)
2. Apply a pressure bandage and immobilize the affected limb.
3. Keep the victim calm and give reassurance.
4. Mouth-to-mouth resuscitation should be applied if breathing becomes difficult or stops.
5. Arrange for emergency services, but do not leave the victim unattended.

CONE SHELLS

After cowries, cone shells are probably the next most commonly collected shell species; they belong to the family Conidae and over 400 species have been described to date. The family is identified by a consistent form resembling an inverted cone with a long and narrow aperture and a sharp-edged outer lip. At the base of the cone is a spire which generally takes the form of a flattened disc with each whorl almost covering the previous one.

Although all cone shells have a well-developed venom apparatus, there are about 10 species which are known to cause severe and even fatal stings to human beings. These are mainly the following fish-eating cones. The aulicus cone (*Conus aulicus*) has a brown shell flecked with triangles of white running from the flattened spire to the base of the shell in two broad horizontal bands. It is one of the largest of the cone shells but is fairly rare. The Great Barrier Reef of Australia is one of the best-known

areas in which it is found. The textile cone (*Conus textile*) is khaki-coloured and marked with dark brown wavy lines which run diagonally across the shell. It is common in the Indo-Pacific region, but is also found in the Red Sea as well as off the Florida coast and in the Caribbean. The marble cone (*Conus marmoreus*) is dark brown to black and is flecked with white which gives the shell its marble look. In some cases the black/brown background is substantially reduced making the shell look almost white. Tulip shells (*Conus tulipa*) are a rather smudged brown and white with underlays of pink. The whole shell is crossed over with spotted lines. Geographer or geographic cones (*Conus geographus*) vary from reddish to dark chocolate brown with white flecks and are among the most poisonous cones. They are found in the Indo-Pacific region.

Other cone shells which are considered to be dangerous to humans include: the agate or tortoise cone (*Conus ermineus*), the cat cone (*Conus catus*), the striated cone (*Conus striatus*), the exceedingly rare glory of the sea (*Conus gloria-maris*) and the pearled cone (*Conus omaria*).

Cones have a proboscis extending from the narrow end of the shell's aperture which is capable of reaching around to most of the shell's extremities; all live cone shells should, therefore, be treated with extreme caution. When the cone attacks its prey, its proboscis extends from the shell and a harpoon, called a radula tooth, is ejected from it and into the victim. The radula tooth is capable of penetrating human skin and in some cases (e.g. the *Conus geographus*) can also penetrate clothing. Venom is injected into the prey, which is then immobilized and engulfed by the snail with its distensible stomach.

The sting from a cone shell varies from being painless to excruciating and is aggravated by salt water. The affected area may become swollen and numb, whitish in colour and blue around the perimeter. This numbness may extend to the whole body within 10 minutes from the sting and may then develop into paralysis within 10 to 30 minutes. Respiratory paralysis may result in unconsciousness and even death. Cardiac failure has occurred but in most cases this is believed to be secondary to respiratory paralysis. The clinical state deteriorates over a one- to six-hour period, after which improvement is likely and full mobility and activity should be regained within 24 hours.

▼ *The cone shell paralyzes its victims using its proboscis.*

CONE SHELL

siphon

proboscis

radula tooth

First Aid

Before paralysis:

1. Immobilize the limb and apply a pressure bandage, with or without a ligature.

2. Keep the victim quiet and rested.

3. Ensure that the patient is lying down with the head lower than the feet, particularly if shock is apparent.

4. Give constant reassurance and do not leave the victim unattended.

5. Call for immediate medical assistance.

After paralysis:

1. In addition to the above also apply mouth-to-mouth respiration. Artificial respiration is the major contributor to saving a victim's life.

2. Apply external massage if the heartbeat is weak.

3. Keep reassuring the patient, who can usually hear but is unable to communicate. Instil confidence.

4. Get medical help as quickly as possible, but do not leave the patient unattended.

CROWN OF THORNS

The crown of thorns is also known as the **sea star** and **venomous starfish**. Injuries from these predators come mainly from people inadvertently treading on them or by divers touching them. Venom is injected into the victim from small sacs situated at the base of spines along the animal's many legs and these spines may remain embedded in the patient. Pain is immediate and severe and persists for several hours before subsiding. Bleeding may be considerable and swelling with inflammation may develop. The regional lymph gland may become tender and swollen within hours. The pain, swelling and a general condition of feeling unwell may continue for months, especially if not all the spines are removed.

As the symptoms diminish, itching may increase. Always wear shoes with hard soles when walking near a reef, gloves when handling the animals and protective clothing when diving.

First Aid

1. Remove all the spines which are easily accessible. Be careful not to break any as they are very brittle; a piece left in the wound will exacerbate the problem.

2. The limb should be immobilized and the victim should be made to lie down and kept calm.

3. Immerse the affected area in hot water as this will relieve the pain and help to break down the toxins.

4. Obtain medical attention as quickly as possible.

▼ *A close-up showing details of the crown of thorns.*

SEA URCHINS

The spines of these echinoderms can cause severe injury. Pain, which can be acute, occurs immediately after penetration and can last for up to four hours. The area around the puncture area may become numb, and inflammation may occur. Black discoloration of the puncture area may last many days and is sometimes mistaken for the spines. Some species, mainly belonging to the family Toxopneustidae, have been known to cause severe generalized pain, shock, respiratory distress and even paralysis. Sometimes reactions may be delayed for up to three months resulting in sea urchin dermatitis.

First Aid

1. Immobilize the limb and remove accessible spines. Urchin spines are very brittle and break off easily if any pressure is placed on them.

2. Bathe the wound with hot water and apply methylated spirits. Rub paw paw (papaya) on the affected area; it is known to have amazing results with certain species of urchin.

3. In the case of *Toxopneustes* victims, keep a close check on respiration and be prepared to assist with mouth-to-mouth or artificial respiration if the patient has breathing difficulties.

SPONGES

While most sponges are innocuous citizens of the marine kingdom, some of them are not. These sponges, of which *Neofibularia* spp., *Tidania ignis*, *Fibula nolitangere* and *Microciona prolifera* are among the more notorious, can cause a contact dermatitis when touched. This dermatitis, which generally develops between five minutes and two hours after contact, causes a stinging or prickly sensation which may degenerate over the following day or two into severe itching.

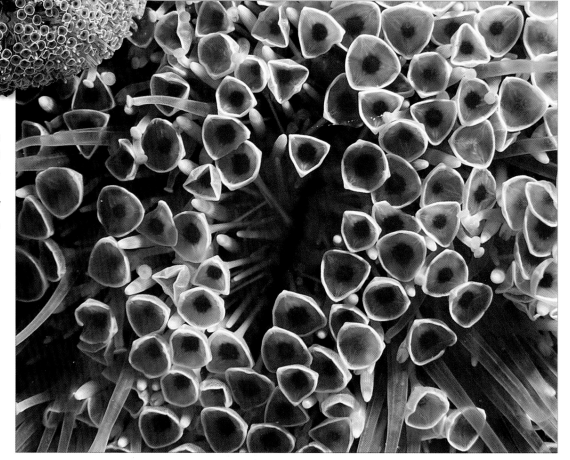

▲ *The toxic flower urchin can have severe effects but death is rare.*

▶ *Flower-like 'pedicellariae' deliver the urchin's venom.*

◀ *Bristle worms cause instant pain which can continue for a few days.*

First Aid

1. Avoid touching the affected area and, above all, do not rub it as this will make it considerably worse.

2. Do not touch any other part of your body or anybody else as it can cause the dermatitis to spread. Do not rub your eyes.

3. Apply methylated spirits to the affected area and a cooling lotion such as calamine, or even cold, preferably iced, water.

4. If spicules of silicon and calcium are present, these can be removed by putting adhesive tape across the affected areas and then removing it; the spicules should come away with the tape.

SEA WORMS

Sea worms belong to the class Polycheata and dangerous species belong to the mainly tropical Amphinomidae, Glyceridae and Eunicidae families. Sea worms occur in the tropical, subtropical and temperate waters of the Indian, Pacific and Atlantic oceans, the Gulf of Mexico and the Caribbean. These animals, which can be likened to an underwater centipede, are elongated and subdivided into segments each of which has a pair of bristles. Their chosen habitat is under rocks or in corals. They cause injury either through penetration by the bristles, or by biting. Contact causes intense itching or a burning sensation which could last for up to a week.

First Aid

1. Remove any bristles by applying adhesive tape across the affected area. Rubbing the area with sand will also help to remove bristles.

2. Apply an acetic acid (such as vinegar) or alcohol, alkalines or dilute ammonia.

3. Apply calamine lotion or any other cooling lotion.

4. Bites should be washed with sodium bicarbonate, salt water or any antiseptic solution.

5. Apply local anaesthetic ointments, gels or sprays, or steroid cream to the affected area initially, to be followed later with an antibiotic ointment.

6. Refer to a doctor.

CORAL CUTS

Many corals have sharp edges and these can cause severe lacerations. The consequences of these cuts or scratches can be as serious as those inflicted by some of the more aggressive marine animals. This is due to the infected slime which covers the coral and the presence of tiny foreign bodies remaining in the laceration, including discharging nematocysts.

Often the laceration, while painful at the time, is ignored because it looks innocuous. However, a few hours or perhaps days later, there may be a smarting sensation which intensifies under hot water. Local swelling may occur with red discoloration and tenderness on light pressure and movement. Eventually a festering sore or ulcer may develop. Alternatively an extremely itchy lesion may result and persist for weeks or even months; this may convert into a scratching-induced neurodermatitis.

First Aid

1. Thoroughly clean the wound as soon as possible after the injury and remove all foreign matter.

2. Apply local antibiotic powder or an ointment such as neomycin.

3. Dress the wound in order to keep it dry.

4. Monitor the injury carefully and see a doctor if there is any sign of deterioration.

CHAPTER NINE

DIVERSIFY YOUR DIVING

Diving is an exciting and rewarding form of recreation, and the sheer thrill of enjoying nature on its own terms is sufficient reward in itself to justify the expenditure and the trouble involved in buying the necessary equipment and undergoing the required training.

However, there often comes a time in a sport diver's career when he or she feels the need to add another dimension to the diving experience. Some of the many speciality activities open to divers include the following:

- Underwater photography and video
- Cold water and ice diving
- Wreck diving
- Cave diving
- Marine research
- Mixed-gas diving

UNDERWATER PHOTOGRAPHY AND VIDEO

If photography is the diving activity you wish to take up, you must begin by asking yourself what your motivation is for doing so, since this will govern the type of photography you follow and the equipment

Nikonos 5 and strobe.

you acquire. If your motivation is to capture colour and form, your choice of medium would be stills photography; if it is to catch movement and action, your direction should lie in video.

Underwater photography, irrespective of the format chosen, requires a special disposition. Attention to detail and a fascination with seemingly small and

Good equipment and techniques are indispensable to good photography.

insignificant things are important, while an eye for colour and composition is a prerequisite for anyone hoping to take exciting and interesting pictures.

It is important when starting out to view your work constructively. Initially, it is enormously exciting to actually get some results when you collect your photographs from the processing laboratory, yet often what looked like a lovely picture underwater turns out to be something that you can hardly recognize as being of this earth when you see it on film. Do not be discouraged; persistence is a key factor in underwater stills photography. Trial and error is ultimately the best teacher, but it is time-consuming and requires a

Fixed-focus waterproof camera.

dogged determination to succeed. Fish do not stay still for long and virtually all have an uncanny knack of knowing that you are trying to take a photograph of them, moving off just when you are about to press the shutter button! Likewise the sea is seldom still, tides and ocean currents create constant motion and the wind agitates the sea's surface. Add to this the effect water has on light quality, colour, distance, refraction and distortion, and a truly challenging scenario presents itself to the aspiring photographer.

▶ *With close-up photography it is possible to capture intricate beauty.*

▼ *For spectacular results, an eye for compostion is vital.*

For the beginner, it is best to start with an 'instant' disposable camera. It is an inexpensive item but is only good for about 2m (6ft) of depth; you can rent a waterproof box which will allow you to use the camera down to 30m (100ft). In some areas, there are auto-dispensers on the beaches which sell disposable underwater cameras. Over time, your camera should evolve into a fully operational system with flash and a choice of lenses.

When choosing equipment, submersible waterproof housings are always an option for your land

camera. They can be bulky, but are strong and reliable and cheaper than amphibious options such as the Nikonos RS-AF. No matter what type of system you choose, it must always be treated with great care. Check that all connections are clean, that 'o' rings are free of dust and that there are no nicks or cuts in the seals. Ensure that the flash fires correctly; with a rechargeable flash, make certain that the recharger works and that it is compatible with the available electrical supply.

Options available to the underwater photographer include wide angle and macro photography – both are challenging and have their own advantages. The skill in underwater stills photography lies in the diver's ability to master the technical factors and to marry these with an understanding of the marine environment and an ability to interpret Nature's kaleidoscope artistically.

With video the challenges are somewhat different, since the capture of movement is its *raison d'être*. Furthermore, with the sophistication of modern technology, it is often possible to end up with a better image than that which the eye actually saw.

Since the point of video for most amateurs is to create a home movie which can be shown to friends, the skill lies in putting together sequences which create a coherent flow of action. Thus, the construction of a storyline before commencing any photography is important and the videographer should develop that storyline with good, apposite photography and the use of accompanying sound

effects, commentary and music. It is important to plan sequences; this may require advance research and a careful selection of dive sites. While shooting underwater, it is vital to stabilize yourself (usually by kneeling on the sea floor while taking care not to damage any marine organisms), and to wait for action to happen about you, rather than to try and swim after it. It is a good idea for your buddy to swim to the other side of the reef and then swim towards you. The fish in front of him or her will automatically find themselves also swimming towards you, thereby making for a more interesting shot.

Choosing the correct system is always a problem and it is extremely difficult to keep up with technology. Virtually all systems are designed for the terrestrial market so waterproof housings are of primary importance. As some housings are rather awkward to handle, it is best to choose a system which already has a good quality housing for sale, such as those made by Sony. Use a tripod whenever possible in order to avoid camera shake. Luckily, there is no wastage with video; you can re-use the tape at any time.

◀▲ *With their colour and form, jellyfish are interesting photographic subjects.*

▲ *In wreck photography, it is important to include recognizable details.*

Flash is essential because of the loss of light and colour distortion underwater.

▲ *Video offers exciting opportunities to capture life and movement underwater.*

▲▲ *A combination of ambience and detail makes for a pleasing picture.*

Both underwater stills photography and videography enrich the diver's underwater experience through the never-ending challenges they present. Both hone the diver's observation skills and knowledge of marine animals and both require a disciplined approach to diving. Most training associations run photographic courses and if you are undecided on whether or not you want to become involved in photography or which format to follow, it is advisable to go on a course first as this will give you the opportunity to make an informed decision.

COLD WATER AND ICE DIVING

More invertebrate life is found in colder waters than in the tropical oceans so it is true to say that cold water diving is perhaps some of the most rewarding. However, many people never have the opportunity to visit colder climates and, even if they do, most shy away from cold water diving because of the discomfort involved. Nevertheless, there are just as many cold water diving locations and cold water divers in the world as there are warm. You do not have to visit a coral reef to see brightly coloured fish and animals; the kelp forests of South Africa, California and Scotland are legendary and these, together with magnificent underwater rock and cavern formations, considerably enhance the diving experience. In addition, some of the best-preserved wrecks in the world are located in cold water while one of the greatest concentration of shipwrecks is found in the Orkney Islands off the north coast of Scotland.

The term 'cold water diving' describes any area which necessitates the wearing of some form of insulating suit, and also encompasses all diving techniques applicable to divers submerged in water below 10°C (50°F). Obviously, the temperature of the body will fall the longer a diver stays submerged. The rate at which it drops is dependent on the temperature of the water, the time spent at depth and the degree of insulation provided by the diver's suit. It does not matter what type of dry suit you have as long as it keeps you dry and enables you to wear insulating layers of clothing underneath.

In extreme cold, the diver should also wear a set of dry gloves and a neoprene or latex full-face cover, plus a full-face mask to minimize the skin's exposure to the outside elements. It is also a good idea to wear a scarf inside your dry suit.

The danger of hypothermia increases if repeat dives are made before the diver has had a chance to fully rewarm between dives; it is essential that an experienced dive marshall is on hand to assess the continuing dive programme.

Once out of the water, there is a very real danger of wind chill further reducing the body's temperature to a dangerously low level. This can be prevented by the diver inflating his dry suit with air once on the surface, thereby adding a further layer of insulation. A thermal top covering of some kind is necessary for long boat journeys and something warm should be worn on the head and hands.

◀ *Crystal-clear waters await divers beneath the ice.*

Ice diving, that is, under sheet ice, is potentially very risky and particularly challenging. This type of dive normally occurs in fresh water or in latitudes where the climate is so constantly cold that the sea has frozen. One of the great advantages to diving under ice is that, once the surface has frozen over, the water is unaffected by wind or weather and all sedimentation quickly settles leaving the water crystal clear. Even in extreme cold, there are many signs of marine life and divers may have rewarding encounters with seals as well as explore shipwrecks encrusted in gorgonian sea fans and soft corals.

Divers should treat ice diving as something akin to cave diving: the 'safety net' of being able to come to the surface and receive fresh air in an emergency is lost. True ice diving takes place under ice that is capable of carrying the weight of people walking on it – at least 15cm (6in) thick. A hole large enough to take two divers is cut into the ice and the divers should never venture into it without a separate safety line securely tied between each diver and their tenders on the surface. For safe ice diving a minimum of six divers is required: two are the initial, or advance divers, two are safety divers and two are surface tenders. An additional safety requirement is to mark the underside of the hole with a flashing strobe light. Equipment should be of a very

high standard and designed not to freeze under any conditions. The freezing-up of a regulator while under the ice could be catastrophic and result in death or permanent injury to the divers involved. Predive planning is essential and a properly qualified supervisor must be on hand at all times.

There are a number of ice-diving locations for recreational divers and any of the major diving organizations should be able to provide details about the various options. Norway and Sweden are an obvious choice; there are also a few centres in Alaska. All the centres offer courses and instruction to a high degree of safety. To dive the great ice sheets of the Arctic and Antarctic involves considerably more planning and cost. This type of diving is usually done by scientists undertaking specific research.

▼ *Scottish waters are some of the best in which to experience cold water diving.*

▲ *It is not only the ancient remains of ships that wait to be explored by wreck divers!*

▶ *In the twilight world beneath the surface, wreck divers have the chance to explore history.*

WRECK DIVING

Marine archaeology and wreck diving offer the diver an opportunity to explore history. There is a certain romance associated with the earlier actions of humankind, whether they be the submerged remains of an earlier civilization, the debris of an accident at sea, or the stark and grim results of war. These mute memorials leave the diver to decipher events from the silent, corroding metal and splintered wood that the sea steadily, inexorably reclaims for itself. Herein lies the fascination of wreck diving.

Academic discipline has been introduced to the subject and from this the science of marine archaeology has developed. Recreational divers interested in this field can make a major contribution to the research and understanding of our maritime history. In order to obtain the necessary skills, special training courses are offered by all the major international scuba diving training associations, as well as national diving associations and diving clubs. To pursue an interest in marine archaeology it is necessary to join a diving group which specializes in this field of activity. It requires a certain dedication and commitment, involving research in libraries, maritime archives and related sources as well as diving in areas where conditions are frequently adverse and unpleasant. One drawback is that it is area-specific, thus its regular pursuit is only possible in diving areas where there has been a history of maritime activity or where there is a wreck of significance.

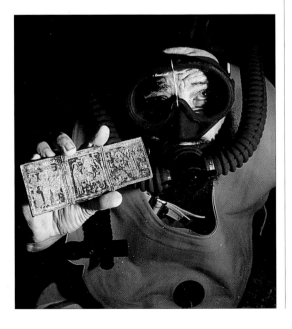

CAVE DIVING

Cave diving is not for everybody. Some people love diving under and around rocks and overhangs and through narrow chimneys into large caverns – all the time surrounded by a curtain of absolute darkness broken only by the stubby beam of the diver's torch. There is an enormous feeling of expectancy and for the more imaginative, there is the prospect of perhaps coming across some long-lost treasure hidden by bandits of a previous era.

Descending into the black abyss that seems to stretch into the very bowels of the earth is a sensation that excites many cave divers. Both freshwater and salt-water cave or cavern diving can be exciting and different but dangerous: it is a tragic reality that many cave divers have lost their lives or come close to it. Research has revealed that the main reasons for this are the following:

1. Inadequate training. An Open Water diving certification is not sufficient for cave diving; specialized training is required in order to prevent accidents from happening.

2. A continuous guide line to the surface must be used at all times, no matter how innocuous the cave may seem.

▲ Care must be taken in cave diving not to become entangled in roots and debris.

◄ Clearance must always be given from the necessary authorities before anything can be removed from a wreck.

▲ *Cave diving is exciting but it is not for the squeamish!*

▶ *A cave diver carrying the mandatory three light sources.*

▶▶ *Mixed-gas diving is being increasingly used by scientists doing underwater research.*

3. Each diver should have at least three independent sources of light. Although the water in many cave systems may rank as the clearest in the world, it becomes the blackest of inks when the lights go out.

4. Cave diving should be restricted to a maximum depth of 40m (130ft). Depth has probably claimed the lives of more divers than anything else, due to narcosis, decompression sickness and cold.

5. Two-thirds of the air supply must be reserved for the return to the surface and all divers must return at the same time (ie: when the first diver uses up a third of his or her air supply). Air rules are extremely important and must be rigidly applied when diving in any enclosed environment.

Under no circumstances should cave diving be attempted without formal training by a registered cave-diving instructor.

MARINE RESEARCH

Here the emphasis is not on diving, but rather on the collection and retrieval of information from an underwater site in a systematic and scientific way. The main purpose of amateur divers involved in research is to assist professional scientists in the collection of data.

It is important for research divers to be experienced and well trained. Improper research or collecting techniques could invalidate the assignment as, once a marine site has been disturbed, there is seldom a second chance to obtain primary data. For a diver to participate in this form of diving activity it is necessary to become a member of a team. Membership is usually initiated by the diver's interest in a particular subject.

MIXED-GAS DIVING

The purpose of mixed-gas diving is to extend both depth and bottom time. By reducing the quantity of nitrogen in the breathing gas (by proportionately increasing the ratio of oxygen) the dangers of nitrogen narcosis and decompression sickness are lessened because of a correspondingly reduced uptake of nitrogen in body tissue.

However, because of the risk of oxygen toxicity when oxygen is breathed at a partial pressure greater than 1.4 bar(a) or 1.6 bar(a) at rest, there is a limit to which oxygen can be used to dilute nitrogen in any breathing gas. Depending on the desired diving depth and duration of bottom time required, various proportions of oxygen and nitrogen (Nitrox) are mixed.

Nitrox has been used for many years by military and commercial divers and, more latterly, by scientific divers; it is also becoming increasingly popular among recreational divers.

Trimix, a breathing gas that combines nitrogen, helium and oxygen, is also being increasingly used. Here, helium is introduced to further reduce the quantity of nitrogen, thereby reducing the risk of nitrogen narcosis at greater depths.

Mixed gas broadens the parameters within which diving can take place and it is predicted in many diving circles that it will become the breathing gas of choice for dives between 12–45m (40–150ft) in the future. However, it should not be attempted without formal training and proper knowledge of all the risks involved.

GLOSSARY

ABSOLUTE PRESSURE: Total pressure exerted at any point, including atmospheric and hydrostatic pressures.

AIR EMBOLISM: The blockage of a blood vessel by an air bubble as a result of a lung expansion injury.

ALVEOLUS: A small membranous sac situated within the lung at the end of the respiratory system within which gaseous exchanges take place.

AMBIENT PRESSURE: The pressure surrounding an object.

ANOXIA: A complete lack of oxygen in the blood.

APOGEE: The point of the moon's orbit which is furthest from the earth.

ARCHIMEDES' PRINCIPLE: When an object is partially or wholly immersed in a liquid it is buoyed up by a force equal to the weight of the liquid displaced by that object (*see* buoyancy).

ASPHYXIA: A restriction of the airway which results in the cessation of oxygen and carbon dioxide transfer to and from the body.

ATMOSPHERIC PRESSURE: The pressure of the atmosphere exerted on the surface of the earth, which is equal to one bar or 14.7 psi.

BACKWASH: The flow of water back to the sea following the carrying of water onto the beach as a result of wave action.

BALANCED VALVE: A valve that does not require added force in order to open or close it to control pressure.

BAR: A measure of hydrostatic pressure which is equal to atmospheric pressure.

BAROTRAUMA: Physical damage to the body as a result of changes in pressure and volume.

BOURDON MOVEMENT GAUGE: An instrument that uses a curved metal tube to indicate pressure.

BOYLE'S LAW: At a constant temperature, a volume of gas will vary inversely with absolute pressure while the density will vary directly with absolute pressure.

BRONCHI: Small tubes which connect the trachea to all sectors of the respiratory tract.

BUOYANCY: The upward force within a liquid exerted on an immersed or floating body. *Negative* buoyancy indicates that the upward force of the liquid is less than the downward force exerted by the body, and *positive* buoyancy occurs when the upward force of the liquid is greater than the downward force of the body. *Neutral* buoyancy occurs when the upward and downward forces exerted on the body are in balance.

CAPILLARIES: Tiny blood vessels that join arteries to veins in the body.

CAROTID ARTERIES: The main arteries supplying blood to the brain.

CEILING: A depth, indicated by a dive computer, above which a diver may not ascend safely without decompressing.

CHARLES'S LAW: At a constant pressure, the volume of gas will vary directly with the absolute temperature.

CLOSED-CIRCUIT SCUBA: An underwater diving system in which all exhaled breath is recirculated within the system, filtered and rebreathed.

CORIOLIS EFFECT: The deflection of winds and currents caused by the rotation of the earth.

CYANOSIS: A bluish discoloration of the skin due to insufficient oxygen in the blood.

DALTON'S LAW: In a mixture of gases, each gas exerts a pressure proportional to the percentage it represents of the total gas.

DECOMPRESSION SICKNESS: The accumulation of nitrogen bubbles in the tissues caused by a rapid reduction of pressure. Also known as *decompression illness*, the *bends* and *caisson disease*.

DEHYDRATION: The abnormal loss of fluids from the body.

DIURESIS: Fluid loss due to excessive excretion of urine.

DIURETIC: A substance that increases the output of urine by the kidneys.

DIVE TABLE: A set of tables produced to indicate the maximum periods permissible at different depths and the corresponding decompression stops required.

DOWNSTREAM VALVE: A valve that opens in the direction of gas flow.

DUMP VALVE: A manually operated exhaust valve on a buoyancy compensator that enables air to be expelled quickly.

EBB TIDE: An outgoing tide.

EMBOLUS: A blockage carried in the blood from one vessel into a smaller one resulting in a restriction of circulation.

EPIGLOTTIS: A thin cartilage plate that folds over and protects the windpipe during the act of swallowing.

EPILIMNION: The warmer layer of water above a thermocline.

EUSTACHIAN TUBE: The tube or canal which connects the throat to the middle ear, thereby enabling pressure within the middle ear to be equalized with ambient pressure.

FETCH: The area over which wind blows in the process of generating waves.

FLOOD TIDE: An incoming tide.

FRENZEL MANOEUVRE: A method of equalizing pressure in the middle ear.

GAUGE PRESSURE: Pressure reflected in a pressure gauge which uses atmospheric pressure (one bar) as a zero reference.

HALOCLINE: The interface between waters of different densities, especially between fresh water and sea water.

HYPERCAPNIA: An excess of carbon dioxide in the blood which results in the overtriggering of the respiratory system.

HYPERTHERMIA: An increase in core body temperature.

HYPERTONIC: A solution that is saltier than blood.

HYPERVENTILATION: Excessively rapid and deep breathing which lowers the carbon dioxide level in the body.

HYPOCAPNIA: When the carbon dioxide level in the body is below normal.

HYPOLIMNION: The colder layer of water below a thermocline.

HYPOTHERMIA: A drop in core body temperature below 35°C (95°F).

HYPOTONIC: A solution that is less salty than blood.

HYPOVENTILATION: Inadequate ventilation of the lungs.

HYPOXIA: Low oxygen levels in the body.

INGASSING: The process of a gas dissolving into a liquid.

K-VALVE: A Scuba cylinder on/off valve that does not have a reserve mechanism.

LARYNGOSPASM: A spasm of the larynx resulting in the blockage of the airway.

LONGSHORE CURRENT: A current that flows parallel to the shore in the surf zone, due to surf approaching the shore at an angle.

NEAP TIDES: The tides having the minimum range between high and low water.

NITROGEN NARCOSIS: A state of stupor, often euphoric, produced by the narcotic effect of nitrogen in the body under pressure.

OCTOPUS: An extra second stage attached to a scuba regulator.

OPEN-CIRCUIT SCUBA: A self-contained underwater breathing system in which air is inhaled upon demand from a cylinder and exhausted into the water.

OUTGASSING: The process by which a gas that was dissolved in a liquid returns to its gaseous state.

OXYGEN TOXICITY or POISONING: A serious condition that results from breathing oxygen at increased partial pressures.

PARTIAL PRESSURE: The pressure exerted by each individual gas within a mixture of gases.

PELAGIC: Marine life belonging to the upper layers of the open sea.

PERIGEE: The point in the moon's orbit when it is nearest the earth.

POLYP: Sedentary cnidarian with a tubular body shape surmounted by tentacles.

RESUSCITATION: The revival of a patient who is not breathing and/or has no pulse.

RIP CURRENT: When water in a surf zone is funnelled through a narrow gap, a strong narrow current is formed which moves away from the shore.

SATURATION: The state that is reached when body tissue has absorbed an equal volume of gas (i.e. become saturated) as that carried in solution in the blood, thus reducing the pressure gradient to zero.

SCUBA: Self-Contained Underwater Breathing Apparatus.

SHALLOW-WATER BLACKOUT: Unconsciousness resulting from a drop in oxygen levels below those required to maintain consciousness. It generally occurs following or during a snorkel dive to depth.

SKIP BREATHING: Holding one's breath between breathing while Scuba diving.

SPRING TIDE: The tide having the greatest range between high and low water, caused by the sun and moon being aligned.

SQUEEZE: A condition affecting the air spaces of the body that occurs when pressure is not equalized. Also known as *barotrauma of descent*.

STRANGULATION: The forceable obstruction of the airway by external compression.

SUBSTRATUM: The underlying base forming the floor of the sea.

SUFFOCATION: The breathing of gas with inadequate levels of oxygen resulting in a loss of consciousness and possible death.

SURF ZONE: The area in which waves break and the water moves forward in the form of surf.

SURGE: The back-and-forth subsurface movement caused by waves.

SWELL: The low, rounded wave form in which energy is transferred through water.

THERMOCLINE: A horizontal and abrupt transition from a warmer layer of water to a colder layer of water.

TOYNBEE MANOEUVRE: A method of equalizing pressure in the middle ear.

TRIM: The control of the body's position or attitude underwater.

TYMPANIC MEMBRANE: Eardrum.

UPSTREAM VALVE: A valve that operates against the direction of gas flow.

UPWELLING: The rising up of water and the subsequent replacement of that water from beneath, caused by offshore winds blowing across the surface.

WAVE: The energy that is created by wind moving through water. The *length* is the distance between two successive waves, the *period* is the time required for two successive waves to pass a fixed point, and the *trough* is the lowest point of a wave.

ZOOPLANKTON: Plankton consisting of minute animals.

ZOOXANTHELLAE: Algae found within the body tissue of hard coral polyps with which they have a synergistic relationship.

INDEX